Dawn of the Divine

Swami Pranavamritananda Puri

Dawn of the Divine

Swami Pranavamritananda Puri

Mata Amritanandamayi Center
San Ramon, USA

Dawn of the Divine

By Swami Pranavamritananda Puri

Published by:
Mata Amritanandamayi Center
P.O. Box 613, San Ramon, CA 94583-0613
USA
www.amma.org

First Printing by MA Center: April 2017
Address in India:
Mata Amritanandamayi Mission Trust
Amritapuri, Kollam Dt.
Kerala 690546, India
www.amritapuri.org
inform@amritapuri.org
Europe: www.amma-europe.org

Dedication

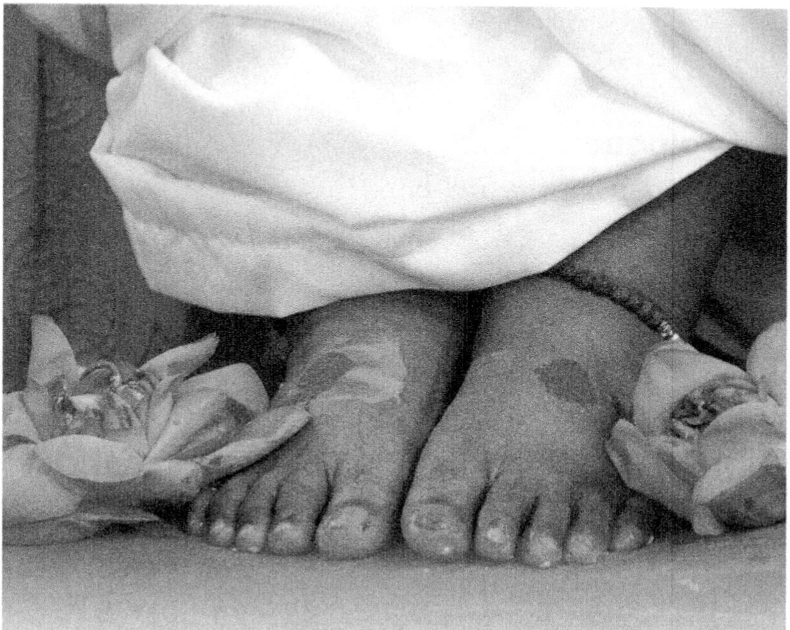

This book is dedicated in all humility to
my most beloved Mother and Master,
Śrī Mātā Amṛtānandamayī Dēvī.

contents

acknowledgments

I remember with gratitude all those who have contributed to make this book see the light of day.

Prologue
"Guess what's in my hand?"

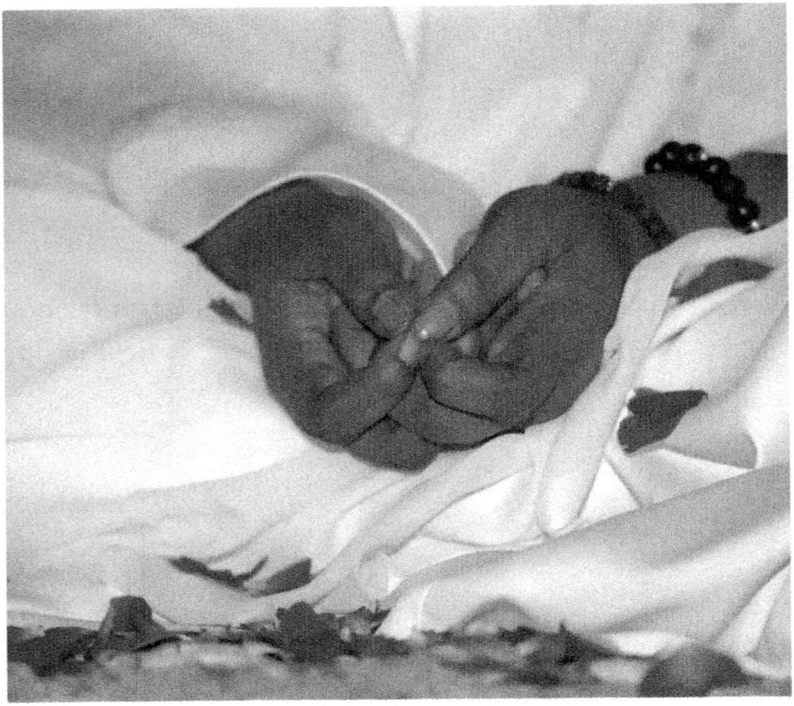

There was a man who used to make his living by selling eggs. A friend hid an egg in his hand, held it behind his back, and asked the egg seller to guess what was in that hand.

"Give me a clue," said the egg seller.

The friend gave him several. "It looks like an egg. It has the shape and size of an egg. It's yellow and white inside. It's liquid before cooked. It becomes hard when heated. It's laid by a hen."

On hearing this, the egg seller confidently replied, "Oh, I know what it is! It's some kind of a cake, isn't it?"

Sometimes, we miss the most obvious things. Sages say that God is the most obvious thing in the universe, because He is everywhere, in all names and forms. Our very life is proof of His presence as divine consciousness within us. However, our murky minds and misconceptions veil this naked truth.

Suppose you have been fervently praying to Amma for a very long time, and finally She appears before you in flesh and blood. You cry and ask Her, "Amma, why didn't You come to me earlier?"

Amma replies, "My child, I was always with you, but you couldn't recognize me. I was present in the form of your family, friends and in all other beings. At least, from now on, try to see every being as me in a different form."

For most believers, including devotees of Amma, the universe is marked by a theological duality: God and the world. Devotees of Amma see themselves as part of the world, and Amma as one with God. Only the latter part of the equation is correct. In the true spiritual sense, we are all God, whether we realize it or not. God is all there is. '*Brahma satyam jaganmithyā*' ('Brahman, the Supreme, is the reality. The world is illusory'), declared Ādi Śankara, the most famous proponent of *Advaita*, the philosophy of non-duality.

But we have become so infatuated by names and forms that we miss the nameless and formless essence. We miss the forest for the trees, the gold for the ornaments, and the ocean for the waves – such is our existential lot. Our defective vision, which cognizes only the parts but not the whole, has perverted our understanding. Because we are so identified with names and forms, the world is, for us, a place of bewildering diversity. Alas, we do not perceive the underlying unity, which Amma does.

She has hinted as much: "I am not (confined to) this five-foot-tall body." Yet, despite such hints of Her omnipresence, we fail to notice Her. Not only that, we do not understand Her properly most of the time.

Many years ago, when some of the āśram buildings were being constructed, I was standing near the *kaḷari* one day when I overheard a conversation between two middle-aged men walking along the adjacent lane.

The first man said, "Look, the money for all this comes from abroad."

Second man: "There is a cave behind the temple (kaḷari) here. A tunnel in that cave leads to the sea, which is where all the money comes from."

I went up to the men and offered to lead them to the cave so that they could see for themselves. Though taken aback by my offer, they accepted. The cave was pitch-dark. They lit a matchstick and saw a man immersed in deep meditation. They did not find any tunnel. The two men felt ashamed about what they had said of the āśram. All they had seen in the cave was someone trying to earn spiritual wealth honestly. Before leaving, they prayed in front of the temple to be forgiven for their mistake.

The world's understanding of Amma often leaves a lot to be desired. A few years ago, when an ardent devotee of Amma died, some critics remarked, "Where was Amma? Could She not have done something to save him? He did a lot of *sēva* (selfless service) for Amma!"

Birth and death are like the two sides of a coin. Laughing at birth and crying at death are akin to considering only one aspect of existence. To expect Amma to save someone, even a devotee, from death is to ignore the laws of nature, which even God-realized souls uphold as sacrosanct. According to Amma, spirituality does not teach one to turn away from death, but to face it fearlessly with a smile.

A few anecdotes associated with the life of the eccentric saint Nārāṇattu Bhrāntan ('lunatic of Nārāṇattu') are worth recounting here. He would push big stones up a hill and then watch gleefully as they rolled down. He was not acting under any Sisyphean curse; rather, his action conveyed the point that it is difficult to advance spiritually but easy to incur a downfall.

One night, Nārāṇattu Bhrāntan went to a cremation ground. It was chilly, and the fire from a funeral pyre provided some warmth. Nārāṇattu Bhrāntan lay down next to the pyre and slept. After a while, he heard shrill cries. When he opened his eyes, he saw Goddess Bhadrakāḷī standing before him in all Her terrifying regalia – matted hair, red eyes, fanged teeth, red tongue hanging out of Her mouth, a garland of skulls, and a girdle of human heads and fingers. Nārāṇattu Bhrāntan was not impressed. When She asked him to leave the place, he did not even bother to reply. He just turned around and continued sleeping. Nothing She did frightened him in the least. Pleased with his fearlessness, Kāḷī offered him a boon, but Nārāṇattu Bhrāntan was not interested. When the Goddess pressed him to ask for a boon, he grudgingly asked Her to increase his lifespan by one second. Kāḷī said that She could not do so. He then asked Her to reduce his life by one second. Once again, She said She could not, for She would not alter the laws of nature. "Well, what boon can you give me?" Nārāṇattu Bhrāntan asked sarcastically. He then asked Her to transfer the elephantiasis that had afflicted his right leg to his left leg. Goddess Kāḷī did so and left.

And yet, *mahātmās* (spiritually illumined souls) have the power to suspend the laws of nature. Years ago, the patriarch of a family of ardent devotees became seriously ill. The doctors' diagnosis was brain fever, and they did not give his family much hope for his recovery. His wife and children were heartbroken. They called Amma, who was in Japan at the time. For two days, while Amma gave darśan to Her Japanese devotees, She was often seen wiping away Her tears. She looked inconsolable, and many people imagined that Amma was crying for the imminent death of the sincere devotee and for the suffering his passing would cause his family. Members of his family pleaded with Amma over the phone to save his life. She consoled them but did not say anything else.

After a long illness, the devotee recovered, much to his doctors' astonishment and his family's joy, relief and immense gratitude. Shortly thereafter, the devotee came with his family to Amṛtapuri. Amma gave the man a very long darśan. She then asked him to have his astrological charts reviewed. When he returned home, he did as Amma instructed. His astrologer said that he was destined to live only until the age of 66. He had just turned 67. Almost 20 years have passed since, and the man is still alive and very dedicated to Amma.

This does not mean that Amma is partial to some. She alone knows the destiny of each being, but being above destiny, has the power to alter that of others. Amma knows what is best for us; we do not. We also know nothing about the laws of karma. Given our severely limited understanding, how can we possibly ask why She intervenes in the destiny of some and not that of others? What can mere mortals like us understand of larger-than-life issues? Hence, let us acknowledge our ignorance of the subtle laws of nature and learn to surrender to the divine will.

It takes a tranquil mind to experience the subtle, multifaceted aspects of life. Our consciousness flows out through our senses on the trail of desires. Physical urges and emotional longings are powerful forces drawing the flow of consciousness away from the center. The right attitude, actions and environment are necessary to make the mind introverted, steady and tranquil. A spiritual master, or Guru, plays a vital role in this respect.

Lorado Taft, the noted sculptor, recounted an incident that took place during a summer camp on the shore of a beautiful lake. The sunsets were exceptionally picturesque. One evening, a young girl asked if she could run home and "show the sunset" to her family. "Certainly," said Taft, "but won't they see it anyway?"

"No," replied the girl, adding, "I never saw the sunset until you came."

The Guru makes reality obvious. The *Guru Gītā*, verses in praise of the Guru, extols the role of the Preceptor thus:

> *na gurōradhikam tattvam*
> *na gurōradhikam tapaḥ*
> *na gurōradhikam jñānam*
> *tasmai śrīguravē namaḥ*
> There is no reality higher than the Guru,
> no austerity more purifying than Him,
> and no knowledge greater than Him.
> Salutations to the Guru! (74)

Lord Śiva even tells His consort,

> *mantrarājamidam dēvi, gururityakṣara dvayam*
> O Goddess, know these two letters ('*gu*' and '*ru*') to be the king of all mantras. (*Guru Gītā*, 107)

One could mine the *Guru Gītā*, other scriptural texts, and the personal experiences of legions of devotees for evidence of the Guru's sublime glory, and it still would not suffice as tribute. We have been singularly blessed to have a Guru like Amma. She does not want anything from us. All that She asks is that we recover our purity of heart and the innocence of a small child.

This book is an offering of select ruminations from my spiritual odyssey. If you are reading this book, you have either heard of or seen Amma and had Her darśan. Amma represents the supreme consciousness abiding in each and every one of us. Let us allow Her to guide us. We will then be witness to the sundown of our ignorance and to the subsequent dawn of spiritual illumination.

1
"What do you think of Amma?"

Amma cannot be explained; She can only be experienced. The following incident exemplifies this point.

Years ago, a distinguished author of many well-known books came to Amṛtapuri. He requested and was granted a personal interview with Amma. Her love and compassion made such an impression that when he emerged from Amma's room, he was glowing with a smile of contentment. I was introduced to this writer. Foolish curiosity prompted me to ask him, "What do you think of Amma?"

The question must have taken him by surprise. After a thoughtful pause, he replied, "What can I say? May I ask you a few questions? What do *you* think of the sky, the ocean and the sun? What do you think of the wind?"

I got his point. Through his rhetorical questions, he was clearly pointing out that natural wonders like the wind and sky are hard to appraise or describe (even though he was a writer!). However, they can be experienced.

Explanation and experience are encounters of different kinds – one is intellectual; the other, visceral. The intellect dissects and interprets according to its fancy. The heart alone can reach the realm of pure experience. Amma is from the ineffable realm of experience.

A comparable incident may be mentioned here. A scholar of some renown once approached Amma and asked, "May I ask you a few questions?"

"Of course, dear son," replied Amma affably.

"Where do all the stars come from? From where do the mountains and oceans arise?"

Amma's smile was captivating. She said, "Son, where do your questions come from? *That* is the source of the entire universe. Seek and discover it."

Rooted in pure awareness, Her response cuts through the daunting demands of erudition to lay bare the simple answer to age-old conundrums. It shifts the focus of attention radically from question to questioner.

Amma does not downplay the role of the intellect, which has its place, but warns against giving it too much importance. When the recondite mysteries of the universe can never be grasped by the intellect, how can the Guru ever be understood? She is one with God, the Creator of the universe, who is even more colossal in His dimensions than the cosmos.

Amma says, "Do not try to judge the Master with your intellect. Your understanding of Him is bound to be wrong. Because you dwell in the mind, and your habits and tendencies are very strong, you cannot understand the Master's 'strange moods' through logic and reasoning. You will fail to understand Him until, at last, it will be revealed to you that the Master cannot be understood through the mind or intellect. You will realize that faith alone is the way. Only through surrender and a child-like openness can one come to know Him."

Many years ago, when I went to Amma's room, I saw Her eating something. She seemed to be relishing it immensely. Amma then put some of it into my mouth. I ate it and then asked, "This is *ñāval* (black plum), isn't it?"

"Don't you remember?" asked Amma.

"Remember what, Amma?" I asked, not understanding what She meant.

"This is the fruit from the *ñāval* tree to which I had tied you."

Amma's remarks revived a dormant memory. About 35 years ago, shortly after I had joined the āśram, I had found some salted mangoes in the kitchen and sneaked some away to eat with rice for lunch. At that time, meals were truly spartan, with no delicious curries to go with the rice. Seeing me walk stealthily away from the kitchen, Amma knew that I was up to some mischief. She sharply called, "Hey, Vēṇu!"

When I heard Amma's voice, I was shocked. Quickly bringing the hand carrying the salted mangoes behind me, I threw the purloined stuff away, and stood guiltily before

Amma, who had, of course, seen what I did. She caught hold of me and tied me to the ñāval tree as 'punishment.' Frightened, I started perspiring profusely. I did not realize then that Amma was only teasing me. Many people, including devotees who had come for Amma's darśan, were watching.

Seventeen years after this incident, Amma told me, "You were very frightened then, weren't you? Actually, I was imagining you as Kṛṣṇa and myself as Yaśodā, and was enjoying the play!" And when Amma was eating the ñāval fruit, She had been relishing the reminiscence more than the fruit. Who knows what mahātmās experience when they interact with the world?

The *Gospel of Śrī Rāmakṛṣṇa* records how Gōpāler Mā, a woman disciple, once brought some confectionery items when she visited Śrī Rāmakṛṣṇa. The moment she entered His room, He asked her, "What have you brought for me? Please give me some of it." Gōpāler Mā hesitated because there were other people in the room, and also because the sweets were cheap. Nevertheless, she offered them to the Master, who ate them happily. He then said, "Why spend money? Make some *narkel naḍu* (confectionery made from grated coconut and jaggery) and bring some when you come here. Or else, bring whatever you cook for yourself – *laushak chacchaḍi* (typical Bengali mixed vegetables), *alu-begun-boḍi diye shojne khaḍar tarkari* (mixed vegetable dish made up of potatoes, eggplant and drum-stick (fruit of the *Moringa* tree)). I cherish items you prepare!"

Gōpāler Mā thought, "What kind of a *sādhu* (holy man) is this? He talks only about food! I'm a poor woman. How am I going to find all these food items? I'll not come here again!"

But she returned because she felt tremendously attracted to the Master and could not keep herself away from Him. She soon realized that Śrī Rāmakṛṣṇa was using food only as a pretext for drawing her close to Him, thus giving her a taste of divine bliss.

Similarly, by eating a ñāval fruit, Amma had blessed me with the delectable pleasure of sweet nostalgia. A mahātmā's actions defy conventional understanding.

The story from the *Mahābhārata* of how Lord Kṛṣṇa saved Draupadi from the dire consequences of incurring Sage Durvāsa's wrath is worth recounting here. During their years of exile, the Pāṇḍavas spent several years in forests. One day, Sage Durvāsa and his retinue of followers called upon the Pāṇḍavas, just after the Pāṇḍavas had finished their lunch. To Draupadi's consternation, there was no food left, and etiquette demanded that guests be regaled with good food. While wondering what to do, Durvāsa said that he and his disciples would refresh themselves with a bath in a nearby river, after which they would eat. As soon as they left, Draupadi prayed fervently. She could not risk incurring the wrath of the sage, known for his flaming temper. He would not hesitate to curse if provoked.

In answer to her prayers, Lord Kṛṣṇa appeared in the hut. Seeing Him, Draupadi confided her problem to Him. After she had finished expressing her sorrows, the all-knowing Kṛṣṇa told her to look once again in the food vessel to see if there was anything left. When she did, she saw a tiny shred of a *cīra* (amaranthus) leaf stuck to the bottom of the vessel. When she hesitantly brought it to Kṛṣṇa, the Lord took it, ate it and expressed immense satisfaction. With that, He left, leaving Pāñcālī (another name of Draupadi) mystified.

In the meantime, Durvāsa and his followers felt strangely satiated. They quietly left the location after their bath, and did not go to the hermitage of the Pāṇḍavas.

When God is satisfied (with even a humble shred of leaf), all living beings are satiated, because He is one with all of creation. How can we ever hope to understand God or the Guru with our puny intellects?

To quote Amma again, "In the modern age, human minds are dry. Too much reasoning has impaired the contemporary mind. People use their intellect for everything. They have lost their hearts and their faith."

This concise commentary on contemporary life is worth contemplating. The internet and the media's fixation on life's superficialities have spawned a glut of information, but alas, we lack a commensurate level of awareness. In spite of our intellectual sophistication, we remain woefully ignorant about our Self. What is the point of worldly knowledge without spiritual wisdom? We might have gained material prosperity, but at what cost? At the expense of the incomparable treasures of joy and contentment, which are our true wealth. We prefer the titillations offered by extroversion to the priceless treasures that introversion yields. Love has become conspicuous by its absence, and negative tendencies like greed, hatred and fear are wreaking havoc in the world. It appears as if the human race is moving toward self-destruction unless it rediscovers the relevance of love and selflessness.

Amma says, "Beauty lies in the heart. Beauty lies in faith, and faith dwells in the heart. Intellect or reasoning is necessary but we should not let it overrule the faith in us. We should not allow the intellect to dry up our heart."

Like a bright yellow dandelion growing between grey cobblestones, Amma's life is strikingly beautiful by virtue of its refreshing contrast from the rampant selfishness of today's world. Her every word and deed brim with selfless sacrifice, love and compassion, and Her dedication to loving and serving others is unconditional. How did so rare a being come to inhabit our world? How has this divine dandelion seeded the spiritual awakening of millions? What is the secret of Her sanctity?

The writer mentioned earlier had difficulty articulating Amma's sublime glory after meeting Her once. As for me, even after spending more than three-and-a-half decades with Her, I still feel incompetent about describing Amma. I dare say that no one will be able to explain who or what Amma is, no matter how long one remains in Her physical presence, for Amma's element is the spiritual, not the physical.

In the *Kēnōpaniṣad*, even the gods Agni, Vāyu and Indra could not apprehend the supernal being that appeared before them but which remained tantalizingly out of reach. Taking pity on them, Goddess Umā appeared when that divine light disappeared, and explained that the venerable presence had been that of *Brahman*, the Supreme. It had manifested to help the gods understand that their power belonged to Brahman, not to them, and that the power *was* Brahman. The fact that they had failed to apprehend the Light was itself a teaching: that God is not something one can apprehend, but is that by which everything is apprehended.

God cannot be explained, but is the power by which one experiences Him. The mind cannot think of God, who empowers the mind to think. The eye cannot see Him, who is the power by which the eye sees. God is not what one hears but the power by which one hears. In other words, the senses or intellect cannot apprehend divine consciousness. Just as one needs a mirror to see one's own face, spiritual aspirants need a Guru to help them behold the Truth.

Goddess Umā was the human face of the Supreme. She assumed the role of Guru to the gods. In this day and age, Amma has incarnated to guide us along the path to the Truth. A true teacher is not only humble but humbling, making us aware of our ignorance. Like a beam of sunlight in a dark room, the Master's words penetrate the deepest recesses of our ignorance. In 1993, clad in a simple white sari, Amma addressed the World Parliament of Religions. Her subject was universal love. There, underlining the essential oneness of all beings, She chanted the mantra for world peace: *'Lokāḥ samastāḥ sukhinō bhavantu'* ('May all beings everywhere be happy'). Her words resonated with the spirit of kinship. Amma continues to conquer hearts with Her disarming simplicity and universal love.

And thus, the hallowed light of *Sanātana Dharma*, India's spiritual heritage, keeps beckoning us, reminding us of our ultimate goal and destiny – to discover our inner unity with the one Self that shines in all as God.

Amma is the self-luminous sun shining in the splendid firmament of Gurus. She is a cool, cleansing, celestial shower that has come to extinguish the burning fire of human sorrow. At the very sight of Amma, sorrows fade away like mist, and people become buoyed up by faith and a bracing optimism. All the sages of yore were great geniuses and practical Vēdāntins. Amma is a living commentary on practical Vēdānta. If we meditate on Her words and actions in the light of scriptural teachings, we will be amazed at their profound wisdom. They are like a commentary on the sacred scriptures; in fact, they *are* the scripture.

"If you carefully watch each and every action of mine, you need not study any scripture," says Amma. Truly, one can learn everything just by closely observing this living embodiment of Vēdānta. What I have observed from Amma's actions is perfection. She lives in every moment, observing everything. She works unceasingly and yet remains detached from everything. And She speaks from Her heart.

Swāmi Rāma Tīrtha, the most notable teacher of Vēdānta to preach in the West after Swāmi Vivēkānanda, spoke of two kinds of sounds: alphabetical and intonational. Alphabetical sound (e.g. language) has meaning in limited circles, whereas intonational sound (e.g. music) has a much deeper and more universal appeal. Amma's appeal is like that of intonational sound; it explains Her sway over people from all corners of the globe who intuit that She can understand the hearts of all, regardless of the language they speak.

It was said of Orpheus that his singing would stop the running brooks and flowing streams. Even animals stopped in their tracks. A lion would halt beside a cow, and a sheep next to a wolf, natural enmity suspended in the magic of Orpheus's music.

Similar is the spell that Amma casts on humanity. She draws all beings to Her bosom. How can one explain it? Why explain it? All that matters is the undeniable elevation and bliss we experience.

2
"Enga? Enga?"

Unlike other babies, Amma did not cry when She was born. This was not because of any congenital abnormality or impairment of the vocal cords. Rather, Her silence suggested a natural-born inner peace, and reflected a sacred harmony between Herself and the world. Ōṭṭūr Uṇṇi Nambūtirippāṭ, the composer of Amma's *Aṣṭōttaram* (108 attributes), paid homage to this phenomenal birth:

> *ōm niśśabda-jananīgarbha nirgamādbhuta karmaṇē namaḥ*
>
> Prostrations to Amma, who performed the miraculous deed of silently emerging from Her mother's womb. (24)

Amma's parents observed that when She was born, the atmosphere was completely silent and peaceful. Not only was She silent, She was also smiling, a smile that exuded profound peace. This silent smile was, in fact, Amma's roaring message to the world – "hush the mind and attain the bliss of the Supreme."

The first thing a baby does on emerging from its mother's womb is cry. Amma says that it appears to ask, "*Enga? Enga?*" – "Where am I? Who am I? Where do I come from?" Ignorant of its spiritual whereabouts and utterly helpless, it can only wail. In contrast, knowledge of the supreme truth makes one smile, like Amma did.

About 5,000 years ago, Kṛṣṇa also smiled when He was born, though born in a prison cell. In that very moment, He conveyed His eternal message, "Keep smiling amidst all sorrows."

Silence is the hallmark of wisdom; it is the gem that adorns the sage. The vignette of a young master seated under a banyan tree and surrounded by old disciples has become an archetype in Hindu imagery. The Master is silent. In his mystic eloquence, the doubts of the disciples are dispelled. The young master is Dakṣiṇāmūrti, regarded as the *Ādi-Guru*, the first Guru, and his disciples are venerable sages.

In recent history, Śrī Ramaṇa Maharṣi favored this mode of teaching. More often than not, his *upadēśa* (teaching) took the form of *mauna* (silence). Many devotees have recorded how their doubts and problems *dissolved* when they spent time in His presence. The silence of a genuine spiritual master is not an absence, but a powerful presence.

To illustrate, Ramaṇa Maharṣi narrates the story of Tattuvarāya. As an act of homage to Swāmi Svarūpānanda, his Guru, Tattuvarāya composed a *bharaṇi* (a type of poem glorifying military heroes), and invited scholars to appraise it. When they heard the poem, the pundits pointed out that the form of the poem was not suited to glorifying a mahātmā; rather, it was traditionally used for paying tribute to an outstanding warrior, one who could kill a thousand elephants single-handedly.

When he heard this, Tattuvarāya said, "Let us take this matter to my Guru." They went to Swāmi Svarūpānanda, and after Tattuvarāya explained why they had come, they all sat down, awaiting the Guru's verdict. The Master did not say anything. Soon, everyone became absorbed in the hushed silence that permeated the very air. Mental activity in everyone became suspended, and it did not strike any of the scholars to press the venerable sage for an answer. The whole day passed in this way. The same thing continued the next day. After three or four days of stillness, the Guru willed His mind to move a little. As soon as he had done so, the scholars resumed thinking. When they realized what had happened, they heaped praises on the Guru. One of them declared, "Conquering a thousand elephants is nothing compared to conquering the rutting elephants of so many egos put together. Only a Guru has the power to do that. Swāmi Svarūpānanda certainly deserves a bharaṇi!"

Silence is not only the highest teaching, it is also the highest form of grace. Amma has repeatedly pointed out that divine grace flows to everyone unconditionally; however, by thought, word or deed, we can create obstacles to that flow. Similarly, silence is a perennial flow of language, interrupted by speech. Speech follows thought, which is preceded by ego. The ego, in turn, is born from misapprehension of individuated identity. Thus we experience a universe of diversity. Before this illusion of names and forms arose, there was only silence. The sublime Upaniṣads emerged from the womb of this pristine silence. Therefore, silence is the original source from which all words arise. If we think words can have an impact on others, we must consider how much more potent silence is.

At present, we are roaming the lowlands of words. In order to attain the pinnacle of Truth, mere mental or physical agility will not suffice. We need to completely subdue the inner chatter and thus recover the pristine silence of the soul.

Amma has pointed out that everything in the world has been defiled by speech, everything except the Truth, that is. According to the scriptures, the Supreme is "*yadvācāSnabhyuditam yēna vāgabhyudyatē*" – "that which cannot be expressed by words but by which words are expressed" (*Kēnōpaniṣad*, 1.5). Amma's silence at birth was a pointer to the supreme truth.

Typically, during a feast, there is a lot of noise, but the moment people start eating, silence reigns. This is an indication of real enjoyment. Inner silence is also the hallmark of all creative work, whether it is writing poetry, painting or singing.

People of real experience do not indulge in idle talk. It is easy to spot the inexperienced; he is like the proverbial empty vessel making the most noise! His tongue goes on wagging, getting rest only when asleep! One who speaks glibly on spiritual matters might fool others into thinking that he or she is learned and spiritually advanced. If only verbal eloquence were proof of one's spiritual elevation!

In contrast, a *jñānī* (knower of the Truth) remains silent. No one has ever heard Amma describing the soul or its qualities in any way. If someone were to ask Her for such a description, She would have to do as the Buddha did – sit in silent meditation with closed eyes. That would also be an answer to the question.

Once, a well-known philosopher, who had hundreds of students, came to see Gautama Buddha. He asked, "Could you say something about the Ultimate, the supreme truth?"

The Buddha looked at him silently for a long time, and then closed his eyes. The philosopher watched him carefully, then bowed down and thanked him, saying, "By your loving kindness, my delusions have been dispelled and I have entered the true path."

One of the Buddha's disciples, Ānanda, had been observing this encounter. Unable to understand what had happened, he asked the Buddha, "What did you do? Had

You answered him, both he and all his disciples would have become Your followers."

The Buddha smiled and said, "A good horse runs even at the shadow of a whip."

To Ānanda's utter surprise, the philosopher and all his disciples returned the next day and took refuge in the Buddha.

The Buddha's cryptic reply is significant. A well-trained horse is so watchful and alert that the mere sight of a whip's shadow makes the horse almost fly. By comparing the philosopher to a 'good horse,' the Buddha was saying that he was totally receptive to learning the Truth. The all-knowing Buddha must have sensed in this philosopher a combination of faith, humility and hope; in other words, an inner spiritual preparedness that made him ripe to receive the learning. And what was the teaching? Silence. The Buddha knew that the moment Truth is expressed in words, it becomes vitiated, and therefore chose to remain silent. Interestingly, the Buddha was also known as 'Śākyamuni' – the silent one of the Śakya clan.

The religious milieu of the Buddha's time was marked by two distinct approaches to seeking the Truth: 1. philosophical inquiries, metaphysical discussions and debates; and 2. seclusion and silence. The two paths were like parallel lines that never converge.

The fact that the philosopher – hitherto walking the path of rational inquiry and metaphysical investigation – had sought the Truth from a votary of sublime silence, *and* assimilated It attests to the limitations of reason and logic. By the philosopher's own admission, the Buddha's was the "true path."

The Buddha knew that the Truth could not be explained, only experienced. It could, however, be shared with someone who had realized the futility of both language and concepts in conveying the Truth.

For the Buddha, silence was the outer face of his inner *sākṣi bhāva*, the witness attitude. His cousin, Dēvadatta, tried to harm and kill Him in many ways. He once sent a mad elephant to crush the Buddha. But on seeing the sage, the elephant suddenly stood still and closed its eyes, as if in meditation. When His disciples asked Him why He did not punish His cousin, the Buddha said, "I must have harmed him in some way in a previous life. If I react now, I will only be accumulating more karma, whereas by remaining a witness, I can break the chain of karma."

At present, our mind is a turbid muddle of thoughts and memories, words and images. Religion aims to make the mind calm and concentrated, like a clear pool of pure water. Once, Amma told me, "Son, we must start practicing stillness at the physical level. One should try to see how long one can keep the body still. When one is unable to do mantra *japa* (repeated chanting), one should try to concentrate on the breath. Concentration may also be practiced by gazing at an open space or any particular point. Try to practice meditation both with the eyes closed and with the eyes open."

We should always practice concentration in one form or the other. Though there are several means, the aim is stillness or silence of the mind. At present, it is only during deep sleep that the mind becomes temporarily still; we forget the whole universe. Remembrance of the world causes sorrow and its forgetfulness leads to happiness.

The *Muṇḍakōpaniṣad* points the way to inner silence and stillness: "The *praṇava* mantra ('Om') is the bow, the Self within, the arrow, and Brahman, the target. The target should be hit by an unerring man, and like the arrow, become one with It." (2.2.4)

Those who have attempted to meditate know that it is not the easiest thing. Most minds are extroverted. When Arjuna laments to the Lord that controlling the mind is akin to controlling the wind, Kṛṣṇa compassionately lets him in on the two secrets to attaining mastery over the mind: *abhyāsa* (unrelenting practice) and *vairāgya* (dispassion) (*Bhagavad Gītā*, 6.35). The order of the terms is significant. Practice comes first. It is futile waiting for the harvest of dispassion to arise when we have not sown the seeds of unrelenting practice. There is no shortcut to detachment.

Once, there lived a mahātmā, who had many devotees and disciples. A priest living nearby did not like the mahātmā, and was jealous of his popularity. One day, when the mahātmā was giving a talk to his followers, the priest came up to him and said, "O so-called mahātmā, I don't trust you and, therefore, am not prepared to obey you. Your so-called disciples and devotees may obey you, but I'm not going to do that. Do you think you are a great soul? I don't believe it in the least. If you really are one, make me obey you."

The mahātmā kept silent and just sat gazing at the priest. After two or three minutes, he called the priest, "Please come here." When the priest went up to the mahātmā, he stood on the left side of the sage, who said, "The left side is for my disciples and devotees. Would you please come to my right?" The priest did as told. Turning to him, the mahātmā said, "See, when I told you to come, you came. And when I told you to stand on the right side instead of the left, you obeyed!"

Such is the power and undeniable charisma of an enlightened soul. Amma says that this potential is in every one of us. All we need to do is to develop it.

Once, someone asked Amma, "What is Vēdānta?"

"Vēdānta is a big smile, my dear son," replied Amma with a smile. 'Vēdānta' literally means 'end (zenith) of knowledge.' Wisdom begins where knowledge ends. When wisdom dawns, one naturally becomes silent and smiles in omniscience.

"Vēdānta is a big smile" – If we think about it, we will understand what Amma means. We can also smile all the time if we are not attached to anything and live in a state of complete desirelessness. Amma, who is always in sākṣi bhāva, perceives and experiences the Truth everywhere. That is why, unlike the rest of us, She did not cry when She was born. If at all She cries, it is for those who are suffering, thus expressing Her infinite compassion. Like a mirror reflecting an image, She receives all and reflects their minds without getting affected in any way. When many of Her children weep copiously, Amma consoles them, saying, "Children, do not cry. Smile and laugh instead." Although laughter therapy is fashionable these days, only a great Guru like Amma, born with the sweet smile of Self-awareness, can guide us to the inner smile and laughter of the true Self.

For us, the world is a reality, often a painful one. That is why we find it hard to laugh wholeheartedly, even with a full set of teeth! The smiles of some are so artificial that we feel we are in the presence of Count Dracula!

Yet others have smiles that are strategic. They wear a smile as cheesy as the Cheshire cat's, believing it to be a useful expedient that will give them entrance into the inner circle of the great. As Edward Gibbon perceptively observed in *The History of the Decline and Fall of the Roman Empire*, "The frequent and familiar companions of the great are those parasites who practise the most useful of all arts, the art of flattery; who eagerly applaud each word and every action of their immortal patron; gaze with rapture on his marble columns and variegated pavements, and strenuously praise the pomp and elegance which he is taught to consider as a part of his personal merit."

In contrast, there is no agenda behind Amma's smile. It is natural, spontaneous, enchanting and sweet. Amma says that life is not a vale of tears. "Life is for laughing and making others laugh. Laugh wholeheartedly, my children!" She repeats this message wherever She goes – in *satsangs* (spiritual discourses) and interviews, while addressing the United Nations or a small group of disciples and devotees.

Amma's embrace is another manifestation of the love and exuberant enjoyment of life behind the smile. Her hug infuses hope in the desperate and destitute, and Her infectious beam sparks a smile of bliss in their hearts. Like

Lord Kṛṣṇa, Amma has an unfading smile on the corner of Her lips. It is a constant among the variables in Her life, and an indication of Her inner experience of perfect contentment.

Amma's commentary on Śrī Kṛṣṇa gives us glimpses into the inner world behind the outer smile, both His and Hers. "Lord Kṛṣṇa was the very personification of bliss. The source of His bliss was detachment. He fulfilled His duties as a witness, without becoming attached to anything. Thus, He was able to pass from one circumstance to another with a smile, with as much ease as moving from one room to another."

As Amma says, happiness is a decision. We can choose to be happy or morose. Once, a thoroughly depressed and disappointed youth approached a doctor. "Doctor, I'm not feeling well at all, neither physically nor mentally," said the young man. The doctor examined him thoroughly from head to toe, and then said that he could find nothing wrong with him. Nevertheless, the doctor gave him some advice, "Listen. The problem is that you have forgotten to laugh. The only medicine you need is laughter. There is a great comedian in town. His name is Grimaldi. Go and see his show and try to laugh heartily. That will suffice for the time being."

"Doctor," replied the young man, "I am Grimaldi!"

In a sense, we are all Grimaldis at heart. We were born crying. Amma quips that we cried at birth because we were ignorant about our true nature, but we should strive to leave the body with a smile. However, only a rare few can thumb their nose at death. According to Amma, "Lord Kṛṣṇa was one such person. In every circumstance of life, His message was 'equanimity, abstinence and happiness.' That was why he was able to remain smiling, even in the battlefield."

The ancient sages and scriptures teach the supreme act of dying with a smile, with a sense of fulfillment. The *Avadhūtōpaniṣad* speaks of the mental state of the liberated thus: "I am blessed, blessed, for I directly experience the Ātman all the time." (30)

If we desire this state of beatitude, then we should perform *sādhana* (spiritual practices). Amma has illumined the path to spiritual enlightenment for us through both practice and precept. She was born to elevate us from mundane earthly existence to the sublime life of divinity. That has been the aim of all divine incarnations and mahātmās. Life is a brief interlude between *ja* and *ma*, i.e. *jananam* (birth) and *maraṇam* (death), which is why life is called '*janma*,' the 'n' denoting its impermanency. Though life may just be a brief spell, during its span, we are called upon to realize *why* we have been born – to realize the

Truth or God. Living a spiritual life helps us to overcome death or the fear of death.

3
"Where did you put your umbrella?"

The Buddha was once asked, "Who is the holiest person?"

He answered, "Each and every hour is divided into minutes, each minute into seconds, and each second into fractions. The one who really lives in each and every fraction is the holiest person in the whole world."

Most of us would probably not equate holiness with complete presence of mind, and yet, if we think about it, the holiest people we know are those with a larger-than-life presence. Those who have seen and met Amma can attest to this.

Living in the present moment seems like the most obvious thing to do, and yet it is evidently the one skill most people lack. Most of us are either living in the dead past or dreaming of some unborn future. By focusing on the present moment whole-heartedly, we can live *intensely*, i.e. without the interference of any tense – past, future or present – because the portal to timelessness is in the present. Indeed, this is what true meditation is – oneness with pure being, sans time and space.

Many children say, "I cannot concentrate." Similarly, many parents complain about their children, "My child is good at this and that but cannot concentrate on studies."

On the one hand, there is nothing surprising about this. With so many distractions – TV, video games, computers, parties, studies, sports, etc. – how can the mind ever focus on one thing? On the other hand, how focused we are when we watch movies, talk ill of others, or express anger. And yet, when we try to meditate, do japa or study, our minds become all too easily distracted. Why? Because we lack interest in or love for it. Where there is interest, nothing is impossible. We think we need artificial aids to help us concentrate when all that is required are sincere effort and unremitting practice. The mind needs to and can be trained to marshal its scattered thoughts and focus on one thing, whenever required. Spiritual practices offer seekers such training. Amma says that religion is nothing but practicing concentration at each and every moment. Unless one pays attention to every action, including the seemingly insignificant ones, one will never acquire concentration no matter how many years one practices meditation.

Once, a woman preparing to go to the market asked her husband to watch the pot of milk on the stove. When she returned, she saw the milk spilled all over the stove. Enraged, she asked her husband why he had not heeded her instruction. The bewildered husband replied, "What do you mean? I kept an eye on the milk, and it boiled over at exactly 10 o'clock!"

We hear but do not listen; we look but do not see; we touch but do not feel; and we think but do not understand.

There is a story about a Zen Master, Nanin, and his disciple, Tenno, who stayed with the Master for many years, undergoing intense spiritual training. Then Nanin sent Tenno away to impart spiritual guidance to others. After staying away for some time, Tenno returned to see his Master one day. It was raining and he had an umbrella with him. On reaching the monastery, Tenno removed his sandals and placed them, together with his umbrella, outside the door of the Master's room. He then went inside and prostrated before Nanin. After exchanging pleasantries, Nanin said, "Tenno, let me ask you a question: where did you place your umbrella? To the left or right of your sandals?"

Tenno was stumped! The truth was that he had not paid attention to how and where he kept his sandals and umbrella. Instead of focusing on the task at hand, his mind had been elsewhere. Understanding Tenno's lack of alertness, Nanin commanded Tenno to spend another few years of training with him.

There are tales of complete mastery over one's mind, too. One is the well-known story from the life of Ādi Śankarācārya, one of India's greatest spiritual luminaries. Though he lived for only 32 years or so, those years were marked by such brilliance that his life continues to dazzle to this day. We can only gaze on, wonderstruck, when we think of the stupendous achievements of this saint. Śankara was not only a *jñānī* (knower of the Truth) and a *bhakta* (devotee), he was also a marvelous poet, keen logician and philosopher of a very high order. He traveled throughout India several times, talking to people, comforting them and setting up various *pīṭhams* (seats of learning). It is amazing that he achieved all these more than 1,200 years ago, when the world was much less developed, with fewer amenities for education and transportation.

During one of his travels, Śrī Śankara met Śaktibhadra, a great scholar from Kērala and author of '*Āścarya Cūḍāmaṇi*,' a Sānskṛt play based on the story of how Śrī Rāma sent His signet ring to Sītā through Hanumān. Śaktibhadra wanted Śankara to review the play and give him feedback. Śankara read the entire work and then returned it without uttering a word. Śaktibhadra did not know that Śrī Śankara was observing a vow of silence at that time, which was why He returned it without comment. Thinking that Śankara was not impressed with his work, Śaktibhadra burned the entire work as soon as Śankara left.

After a few months, Śankara returned to Śaktibhadra's house and asked him for the manuscript of '*Āścarya Cūḍāmaṇi*.' Śaktibhadra was speechless. He told Śankara what had happened – that he had burned the manuscript, thinking that the Master was displeased. Śankara asked, "Can you rewrite the work from memory?"

Śaktibhadra helplessly said, "I cannot, even if I make many attempts."

Śrī Śankara told him to bring some palm leaves and a stylus. When Śaktibhadra brought them, Śankara started dictating the entire work without missing a beat! Such had been His concentration while reading the play that, in one perusal, He had indelibly committed the whole script to memory.

We may feel that this is not possible for lesser mortals like us, but nothing is impossible for one who sincerely tries. We might not be in the same, lofty league as Śankara or Amma, who are *Yuga Gurus*, Teachers of the Age. Nevertheless, we should ask ourselves how such feats are possible for them. The minds of liberated souls are perfectly one-pointed. They are 'clean slates' – pure and free from any kind of bondage whatsoever. Hence, they are able to focus exclusively on one object.

Ages ago, there was a pure and spiritually elevated scholar in India who knew all the Vēdas by heart. When King Alexander invaded India, he wanted to take away all the Vēdas because his preceptor, who knew how priceless they were, had asked Alexander to bring them. The scholar, who was intuitively aware of the king's intentions, taught each of the four Vēdas to his four sons in that interregnum, and then burned away the leaves imprinted with the scriptures because he knew that Alexander was not worthy of the sacred knowledge. In ancient days, knowledge was primarily transmitted orally from generation to generation, and impressed on the memory slabs of individuals. Such was the retentive capacity of people in days of yore.

Amma's memory is also phenomenal. Those who have sung with Her know that Amma needs to hear a song just once in order to reproduce it perfectly even years later. One might well speculate that what Amma has is not memory in the conventional sense; it is not like a hard disk with a huge but limited capacity. Because Amma does not identify with a finite body but rather with the consciousness that pervades the cosmos, Her 'memory' is more like a wide, panoramic screen on which numberless images and words can be projected without affecting the quality of the screen in any way at all. How is She able to recall all those images or words so easily? Because of Her purity. True love flows incessantly from a pure heart. Love is the best mnemonic device. Amma speaks of how a lover always contemplates the form of his beloved, not because he has received training in meditation but because of his all-consuming love for her. Amma finds everything interesting. She is so full of love that She approaches every encounter with utmost love and concentration; hence Her perfect and total recall.

Amma's memory is also more than just a cerebral feat. It is closely allied with Her qualities of loyalty and gratitude. In the early days of the āśram, She would sometimes visit poor devotees, many of whom lived in small huts. They would arrange a part of the hut for Amma to stay in, and the brahmacārīs accompanying Her would spend the night outside, under the canopy of stars. Amma has never forgotten the hospitality shown by those devotees. Sometimes, when they visit, Amma hugs them tightly, and they reciprocate the warmth of Her hug by embracing Amma tightly. Well-meaning assistants standing by Amma's side might try to pry their arms away only to be rebuked by Amma. She would say, "Do you know who they are? They are the ones who gave us food when the āśram was at its most impoverished. Amma can never forget their love and generosity." She will even specify the items they had brought wholeheartedly to the āśram kitchen years ago. It is not that Amma is partial to older devotees; She loves everyone equally. It is that She never forgets the smallest kindness. It is this quality that differentiates Amma's prodigious recall capacities from those of others.

In our own small and humble ways, we also can try to concentrate and pay attention. Let us make an honest effort to do so. To begin with, we can strive to do seemingly insignificant things with *śraddhā* (attentiveness). To give a small example, most of us are guilty of keeping our books or clothes carelessly. We treat our socks and shoes or sandals even worse; if one of the pair is here, the other is somewhere else! Why can't we learn to keep them together properly? Similarly, when we get up from a chair, how many of us bother to put it back properly in its place? When we are in front of the sacred lamp or the altar, our mind wanders to thoughts of food or some TV program. If we learn to focus our mind on the so-called insignificant things, this will never happen.

The greatness of a person can be measured by how he or she does the smallest actions. One's personality may be evaluated by how clean and neat one's living quarters appear to others. When we observe Amma, we will see that Her every action is performed with utmost care, efficiency, purposefulness and mindfulness.

In the closing hours of Amma's 2016 programs in Pālakkāṭ, as Amma was giving darśan to the last few devotees standing in the queue, She suddenly asked for the microphone and then announced, "Children, please clean up the āśram premises before you leave. The swāmi presiding over this place is Praṇavāmṛta. The first thing I gave him when he joined the āśram was the broom! He is very particular about neatness and cleanliness."

The broom is a tool for cleaning. By giving me the broom to clean, Amma was subtly leading me to a purification of my inner environment, too, by enhancing my level of awareness. External cleanliness leads to inner purity. I felt that Her announcement that morning had been symbolic. Amma wants everyone to grow in awareness not only of environmental cleanliness but eventually of the purity of heart, which leads to *ātmaśānti*, the peace of the Self.

Actually, most of us crave the state of awareness, though we may not be aware of it! Think of how popular high-risk leisure activities such as bungee jumping, white-water rafting, skydiving and mountain/rock climbing have become. The media have successfully captured the visceral appeal of the thrill associated with these endeavors. What all these actions have in common is the sense of heightened awareness they offer. Participants report total involvement, a timeless experience of flowing from one moment to the next in a mode of enhanced perception, a liberating sense of freedom, and even a sense of non-differentiation between the self and environment – all of which could well describe the goal of meditation. These transcendental benefits are the holy grail that high-risk adventurers seek.

A devotee once asked Amma, "Is awareness the same as śraddhā?"

Amma replied, "Yes, the more śraddhā you have, the more aware you will be. Lack of awareness creates obstacles on the path to eternal freedom. It is like driving through the fog. You won't be able to see anything clearly. It is dangerous, too, as an accident can occur any time. On the other hand, actions done with awareness help increase your clarity, moment by moment, and thus eventually enable you to realize your innate divinity."

Amma exemplifies total surrender to the present moment. She accepts whatever comes Her way, be it in the form of a person coming for darśan and pouring out his sorrows to Her, or in the form of an administrative wrinkle that needs to be ironed out. Unlike us, Amma finds *everything* interesting, and yet, because of Her inner detachment, is able to experience each moment of life with utmost awareness. Nothing can affect Her inner bliss, which flows as a continuous stream of love towards humanity.

A seeker approached a famous Zen Master and asked, "What is your sādhana? What kind of spiritual practices do you do?"

The Zen Buddhist replied, "I eat when I am hungry, and sleep when I am sleepy."

"What kind of sādhana is that?" asked the seeker. "I do that, too!"

The Master then said, "Really? Many times, you eat because the food is delicious, because you are invited to eat, or because it's mealtime. For many, eating is a habit. I eat only when I am hungry. Similarly, you go to sleep when it's bedtime. You dream when you want to sleep, and sleep when you want to dream. I go to sleep only when I feel sleepy. It's not a habit."

The name of one of the *ṛṣis* (seers) in the Ṛg Vēda is Śraddhā. It appears that the divine word 'śraddhā' has found a perennial place on the tip of Amma's holy tongue.

Let me share an incident that happened in the early years of the āśram. It was mealtime. We were sitting around Amma, eating. Two or three grains of cooked rice fell off my plate. I did not notice it, but Amma did. She said, "My dear son, eat your food with śraddhā. Food is God. It should be honored. Even for a grain to sprout, God's grace is essential. In addition, the sequence of sprouting, growing, bearing corns and becoming cooked rice requires the combined efforts of nature, man, soil bacteria and many other elements. If you have any respect for this mighty, collaborative effort and for God, how can you casually let bits of food fall around?"

I sat still with a ball of cooked rice in my mouth. I could not chew it for some time. Instead, I was assimilating those wonderful words of wisdom. I made a decision there and then never again to drop, even inadvertently, the smallest morsel of food.

Śraddhā, undivided care and attention, is the secret to success in life. One of the names of the Divine Mother is 'Svādhīna-vallabhā' – 'one who has mastery over Her Lord (consort)' (*Laḷitā Sahasranāma*, 54). All women who influence their husbands through love and devoted service deserve this name.

The great saint of Tamil Nadu, Tiruvaḷḷuvar, and his wife, Vāsuki, shared an ideal conjugal life. Until the very end of her life, that noble lady never asked her saintly husband for anything. She was ever assimilating the wisdom issuing from the daily acts and utterances of Tiruvaḷḷuvar. However, when she was about to die, she said, "My lord, pardon me for being inquisitive about a particular act of yours, which has always eluded my understanding. Whenever I served you food, you would keep a cup of water and a needle near the leaf. Why? Please enlighten me."

Tiruvaḷḷuvar replied, "If a grain of rice had fallen to the ground accidentally while you served food, I would have used the needle to pick it up, dip it in the cup of water to clean it, and eat the grain of rice. However, that never happened, because you were always very careful. You are full of śraddhā!"

His praise was soothing to her dying heart. With joy, serenity and a sense of fulfillment, her soul left the mortal body and became absorbed in the infinite.

Interestingly, the word 'śraddhā' also means 'faith.' What is the connection between alertness/awareness and faith? At first glance, the two terms seem contradictory. On the one hand, alertness or hyper-vigilance can create tension. A person with faith, on the other hand, can become complacent and, therefore, lacking in alertness. Thus, there are negative qualities associated with both. In spiritual life, however, one is always in the present moment, and, therefore, alert. And yet, the seeker's faith that God is protecting him or her removes all tension. Hence, alertness and faith are complementary qualities. Total faith liberates one from all anxiety, hence allowing the devotee to live fully in the present.

Possibly, none can match the level of śraddhā that Vasudēva demonstrated when he carried the newborn Kṛṣṇa to Yaśōdā in Gōkula. His śraddhā was multi-dimensional, combining both total attentiveness and unshakeable faith. The dark prison cell was guarded by the best of Kamsa's armed men. Vasudēva and Dēvakī were shackled to the floor. Outside, it was raining heavily, with thunder and lightning heightening the drama. The night was dark. At midnight, Śrī Kṛṣṇa was born, and assuming His celestial form, blessed His father and mother. He then instructed Vasudēva to carry Him to Gōkula and leave Him quietly beside the sleeping Yaśōdā. Then the Lord reassumed His playful infant form.

Vasudēva swung into action. An ardent devotee of God life after life, Vasudēva was śraddhā personified, because he was always meditating on the Lord. He did not pause even for a moment to take stock of the obstacles or potentially dangerous impediments strewn on his path. All that he knew was that he had to carry out the Lord's instructions. Looking around, he saw a basket in a corner of the prison cell and picked it up. He spread his shoulder wrap artfully in the basket. He then picked up the smiling Kṛṣṇa and placed Him inside the basket. Lifting the basket to his head and holding it tenderly with his hands, he walked out of the cell. He was oblivious to the fact that the shackles that had bound him had come loose, and that the heavily locked prison door had somehow swung open. As he walked out, the guards were sound asleep. Vasudēva hardly noticed the deluge or the piercing darkness impeding his progress. He did not even notice the celestial snake, Ananta, protecting him and the divine infant with its hoods. When he reached the Yamuna, which was in full spate, he stepped into the waters, intending to wade across. With his first step, he was ankle-deep; with his second, the water covered his knees. Subsequent steps brought the water up to his waist, chest, neck and mouth. The miracle took place after the next step, when the water rose to the bridge of his nose. As Vasudēva waded in deeper, the water level did not rise, allowing him to continue breathing. One of baby Kṛṣṇa's limbs was hanging low, in line with the bridge of Vasudēva's nose. The import of the story is clear – the threatening waters of *samsāra* (the cycle of birth and death) cannot inundate a mortal soul if he carries the Lord with love and faith.

Amma has reiterated, "A real believer is full of strength, immense strength. Nothing can harm him. All of life's obstacles, whether created by human beings or by nature, will crumble when they hit against the firm and stable faith of the believer."

You might have seen pictures of Viṣṇu lying on His snake, Ananta. The word *'ananta'* means endless and represents the Infinite. Ananta is depicted as a coiled serpent with its hoods turned inwards towards Viṣṇu. It symbolizes the point that one who has turned within and is aware of God enshrined in his heart becomes endless and infinite, like the Lord Himself.

It is also said that Viṣṇu is in *Yōganidrā*, yōgic sleep. Some people make fun, saying, "What kind of God is that, who sleeps all the time?"

Yōganidrā is not sleep as we understand it. For us, sleep means oblivion. In Yōganidrā, there is total awareness and relaxation, which most of us cannot command even when wide awake. In any case, how many of us sleep peacefully all the time? We wake up because we have desires to fulfill. Our dormant *vāsanās* (latent mental tendencies) rear their head when we wake up. Viṣṇu has neither vāsanā nor desire, and so, can remain in the eternal state of repose but with an underlying dynamism that protects everything in creation. Unlike our sleep, characterized by unconsciousness, in Yōganidrā, there is total wisdom and consciousness.

Viṣṇu is also depicted as surrounded by an ocean of milk. This is no ordinary milk. Even if we milk all the cows in the world, we will not be able to create an ocean of milk. Milk here represents *sattva guṇa*, the attribute of serenity, intelligence and purity. The symbolic meaning is that the Lord dwells in a mind that has become calm and pure.

This state can be attained only through meditation. Amma never fails to stress the importance of meditation, and encourages us to make it a cornerstone of our daily activities. Practice daily for at least 10 minutes. You will notice that you gain tremendous energy. You will have the courage to face all the petty problems of life. According to the wise, the moment you say, "I have a problem," it is clear that "I am not the problem." Just remember you are different from the problem; you are the Self. Meditation gives one this perspective.

What really happens when one meditates? Our thoughts are always flowing. This flow takes place along an unmoving foundation, just as a river flows on a stationary riverbed. In other words, all change implies a changeless substratum. However, the flow of our thoughts is so rapid that we miss the gap between successive thoughts. By becoming aware of this gap and thus widening it, we can get glimpses of that changeless substratum. All spiritual practices are aimed at widening this space of silence until we become like the illimitable space (*Ātman*).

When the turbidity of the mind clears, it becomes as transparent as a limpid pool. Such a mind is a powerful tool. To have some sense of what this state is like, all we need to do is observe Amma. The fact that She can listen to a hundred problems and attend to a host of activities simultaneously without ever losing Her poise hints at the deep, undersea calm She must be experiencing. Such is Her complete mastery over the mind that Amma never forgets anything, although She can induce forgetfulness in others. This explains why we tend to forget our list of problems when we are in Her presence. Amma's blissful nature overwhelms us, making us forget our petty problems.

The *Bhagavad Gītā* makes the same point. Lord Kṛṣṇa tells Arjuna,

> *bahūni mē vyatītāni janmāni tava cārjuna*
> *tānyaham vēda sarvāṇi na tvam vēttha parantapa*
> I have had many births, O Arjuna, and so have you. I know them all, but you know them not, O scorcher of foes. (4.5)

In Her mystic song, '*Ānanda Vīthiyil*,' Amma makes a similar point:

> *kōṭiyabdangaḷ pinniṭṭa kathakaḷen*
> *cārusirayil udiccuyarnnu*
> The events of millions of bygone years
> arose within me.

It is only with the Guru's grace that one can fathom the depths of such mystical utterances. How else can one grasp even pointers to omniscience with our limited intellects?

A great master like Amma can read and understand our every thought because Her mind is perfectly balanced and one-pointed. While a number of instances have been chronicled, many have remained confined to the individual devotees themselves or to their immediate circle of family or friends. One such instance that I heard first-hand took place many years ago. An affluent, middle-aged woman came to see Amma for the first time. Possessing all creature comforts, she was apparently free from mundane problems. Yet, she was aware that she lacked peace of mind. In those days, Amma used to receive devotees in a small hut. This lady entered the hut, came close to Amma, and looked at Her yearningly. She prayed inwardly for solace: "Amma, please give me mental peace." She kept repeating this prayer, as if possessed by her inner turmoil. All this time, she did not utter a single word. Yet, in Her overwhelming compassion, Amma understood the devotee's heart. As She took the woman on Her shoulder, Amma reassuringly whispered into her ears, "Dear daughter, isn't that what I am here for?"

It is by such overpowering compassion – not just in its gross form of extending physical or material help to others, but also in its subtler version of discerning worries and apprehensions and responding lovingly – that Amma binds Herself to millions. Her omniscience has been widely experienced by devotees all over the world, yet this begs the question, "Do we remain aware of this fact 24 hours a day? Do we always remember that Amma is with us all the time?"

Amma also uses Her divine insight to correct erring individuals, helping them overcome their lethargy or weaken their vāsanās. A young man used to visit the āśram frequently for Amma's darśan. Once, he sat behind Amma after darśan. Instead of using the opportunity to meditate in Her physical presence, his mind started wandering idly. At one point, he even started wondering why so many devotees were sitting around Amma and wasting their time when they could do something worthwhile. At that very moment, Amma turned around and, looking directly into his eyes, said, "Get up and do some work, you lazybones!" Stunned by Amma's ability to read his mind, he jumped up and ran to the kitchen, where he did some sēva and fed himself as well!

People like Amma are called *'Pratyutpannamatayaḥ'* in Sānskṛt. In other words, theirs is a quick-witted intelligence. All of us have this capacity but we tend to use it in less beneficial ways.

There was a man who did not like another. Intending to mock the latter, he said, "You know, I never believed in Darwin's theory of evolution, which claims that apes became humans through the process of evolution. But when I see your *lovely* face, I am forced to believe it!"

To come up with such jokes and to present it properly require concentration and presence of mind. Some of us may have these abilities but we use it negatively, i.e. in a hurtful or destructive way. Channeling, preserving and using this potential in the right way is spirituality.

When the mind is concentrated and balanced, one does not find fault with others. In a state of perfect equanimity, there is no sense of duality. If there is no duality, whom can we blame?

Many years ago, a handsome young man came to the āśram to see Amma. He had no faith in Her greatness, and therefore, did not bother to prostrate before Her or show any humility. Amma was not bothered at all. She started talking to him in a very loving manner. The young man then egoistically said that he was the chief police inspector of a certain district. Hearing these words, Amma smiled mischievously, as if to say, "I know all about you!" With utmost kindness, Amma warned him, "Darling son, you are going through a very bad time. Be careful." She then kissed him and gave him some *prasād* (consecrated food). He left early the next morning. Almost a week later, one of the āśram residents saw this man's photograph in the newspaper. The headline read, 'Pseudo-police officer in police custody.' The resident rushed to Amma with this hot news. After reading the news report, Amma said, "What a pity! I feel sorry for him."

Only in the heart of a mahātmā can there be total awareness and prescience on the one hand, and unfailing love and compassion for all, even miscreants, on the other.

In China, there lived a great meditation teacher who was an *avadhūta*, one beyond the pale of social norms and niceties. He used to walk along the streets, carrying on his shoulders a sack with various things. One day, a seeker approached him and asked him, "O Master, what is the effect of meditation?"

The Master stared at him for a few moments and then put down his sack. He did not say anything. The seeker understood what the Master meant and said, "Okay! I get it. And then what?"

In response, the Master once again picked up the sack, hauled it onto his shoulder, and walked away.

The Master's actions were highly symbolic. When one beholds the substratum of the universe – i.e. when one realizes God – the ego dies; one becomes relieved of its tremendous weight. The consequence is peace, *śānti*. By putting down the sack, the Master was saying that meditation helps one to be rid of the burden of his ego. By hauling it onto his shoulders again, he was pointing out that once we have eradicated the ego, we can take on the burden of the world with consummate ease.

4

"Do we obey the Master in thought, word and deed?"

The Vēdas declare, "*Ācāryavān puruṣō vēda*," i.e. "One who is blessed with a competent Master comes to know the Truth" (*Chāndōgyōpaniṣad*, 6.14.2). If that is so, why have we still not realized It? After all, we have come under the guidance of Amma.

The bottom line is this: do we obey the Master implicitly in each and every thought, word and deed? There needs to be *total* surrender to the Master. To our rational mind, the word 'surrender' may sound negative. We usually associate it with defeat and humiliation instead of victory and progress. This is a pity because we do not realize how elevated we can become by submitting ourselves wholly to the Master's spiritual discipline. In Amma's words, a Guru's disciplining is like a doctor's treatment of a patient with infected wounds. Cleaning the wound, applying a salve, and bandaging the wound may be painful to the patient. Nevertheless, the doctor continues doing the job until it is finished, ever aware that it is all for the patient's benefit. The patient's submission to the doctor helps to cure him and relieve him from suffering.

Amma says, "Once you have a real master, you should not worry about spiritual experience. Have faith in the Master and follow His words implicitly. Everything will come of its own accord."

What this means is obedience. Many of us think we are devoted to Amma. To find out just how devoted we are, all we need to ask ourselves is, "How much do I obey Her?" A true devotee of Amma is one who honors Her every word.

Amma says that devotion is obedience. Why should we obey or surrender to the Master? Is having a Guru really necessary? It is, if we are intent on God- or Self-realization. Only one who has seen God can lead another to God. The blind can never lead the blind. Amma is like the doctor of doctors. The root cause of the ailment of mundane existence is vāsanās, which are very subtle. They prevent us from acting without prejudice.

For those who think they have free will, it might be shocking to hear that innate tendencies, which are a kind of mental hard-wiring, give rise to pre-programmed responses. Lord Kṛṣṇa says as much: "*Svabhāvastu pravartatē*," i.e. every creature acts according to its nature (*Bhagavad Gītā*, 5.14). The following story illustrates how powerful vāsanās are.

A scientist spent several years researching the possibility of transmuting plain water into petroleum. He knew that the transformation was possible with an appropriate catalyst. He tried many different materials, but even after several iterations, he could not perfect the formula. He also tried to find ways and means outside the laboratory. It was then that he heard about a lama in the high mountains of Tibet who had knowledge of the catalyst he sought. However, in order to meet the lama, he had to fulfill three conditions:

1. go alone to meet the lama;
2. travel barefoot on the hazardous and tiring journey; and
3. if he succeeded in fulfilling the first two conditions and arrived to see the lama, he would be allowed to ask only one question.

Notwithstanding these stringent stipulations, the scientist decided to go. He traveled barefoot all alone, overcoming all the hardships of the journey. Finally, he reached the abode of the lama. When he was ushered into the lama's presence, he was astonished. Instead of an old, wizened and bearded man he had thought the lama would be, he saw a drop-dead gorgeous woman, who could have easily won the Miss Universe title. Who would have thought such a beauty would be a lama! The attractive woman smiled at him and spoke bewitchingly, "Congratulations, traveler! You have finally reached me. Now, what is your one question?"

Mesmerized by her allure, the scientist instinctively asked, "My dear, are you single or married?"

Vāsanās are not only difficult to overcome, they also distort one's perception of reality. They are like colored lenses that prevent us from beholding the world as it is. These lenses distort our perception, leading us to make wrong interpretations. Only a person like Amma, i.e. one with supreme realization, can eradicate the vāsanās. The Truth is revealed when we go beyond all vāsanās. Hence, it is essential to obey and surrender to the Master.

One day, a renowned scholar of unsurpassed erudition visited the court of a king. After the king received him with honors, the scholar said that he had come with a challenge: to see whether anyone in this kingdom could defeat him in a debate.

The king was in a dilemma. In desperation, he turned to his minister to help him find someone who could save him from ignominy. The wise minister went out, found a drunkard, and persuaded him to present himself at the palace the next morning at a certain time. The minister assured him that he would not have to do any work; all he had to do was to appear in the palace.

The next day, the drunkard appeared at the appointed hour. The minister instructed him not to speak during the upcoming debate, and instead communicate through gestures alone; he could speak thereafter. When the pundit arrived, he was taken aback to see that someone had accepted his challenge. He was also put off to find that his opponent did not talk. When told that the latter was observing a 'vow of silence' on that day and would respond only by gesticulation, he accepted the terms of the debate.

The battle of wits began. The scholar held up one finger. The drunkard responded by showing two fingers. The scholar was amazed. He indicated '3' with his fingers. Intensely irritated, the drunken 'pundit' retorted by showing four of his fingers, much to the scholar's bewilderment. The scholar started perspiring. Here was someone greater than he! In desperation, he held up five fingers. Seeing this, the drunkard was beside himself with rage. He held up six fingers, after which he drew a circle in the air with his fingers. This was too much for the pundit. Acknowledging defeat at the hands of a superior scholar, he fell reverentially at the drunkard's feet. All his pride and ego were deflated, and he sat down a humbled man.

The king was pleased. After bestowing honors on both the drunkard and the pundit, everyone in the court expressed a keen desire to know what had happened; they had not understood the exchange of gestures at all!

The pundit spoke first. He was all praise for the erudition of the inebriated 'scholar.' He explained that he had begun by showing '1' to indicate that everything in the universe is one, that there is only one absolute truth. The opponent had disputed the point by pointing out two entities, *viz.* the *jīvātmā* (individuated soul) and *paramātmā* (Supreme soul). In response, the pundit had held up three fingers to indicate the *triguṇas*, the three interdependent modes or qualities of nature. The intoxicated opponent had revealed a higher truth by showing four fingers, thus alluding to how everything was based on the four Vēdas. The scholar then decided to indicate the five senses of perception, which form the basis of experience. Even there, the 'spirited' man bested him by holding up six fingers to point out that there was, in addition, a sixth sense – the mind, as the *Bhagavad Gītā* proclaims. "He is truly a realized soul," concluded the pundit. He then said, "However, I am totally at a loss to explain the meaning of the circle he drew."

After the scholar left the palace, it was the drunkard's turn to explain. Dispensing with the show of silence, he drawled, "When that man showed me '1,' I knew he was saying that he could drink a bottle of alcohol easily. One bottle? C'mon, that's child's play! I can down two bottles any time! So I showed '2.' Then that impudent fellow challenged me by indicating that he could do better; he showed me '3.' I got angry. Anyone who challenges me in drinking is asking for trouble. So I warned him by showing '4.' And guess what that upstart did then? He indicated '5' bottles. What cheek! I'm not one to take a challenge lying down. That's why I indicated that I was ready to down six bottles!"

When asked about the significance of the circle he had drawn, the drunkard replied, "Oh that! I was trying to say that I can easily drink six bottles if there is *pappaṭam*[1] to go with the drinks!"

Moral of the story? That we assess and evaluate the world according to our mental tendencies, personal experiences and perspectives.

It is extremely difficult to overcome the tendencies of the mind. To do so requires guidance from a Master like Amma and sustained practice on our part. The potency of a Guru's grace and presence can never be overstated. Amma's love is so disarming that She could transform the most diabolical being into an angel. If a devil were to meet Amma, he would be transformed into Swāmi Devilānanda!

During Her first visit to an Indian city in the late 90s, a large crowd turned up for Amma's darśan. The men's queue was long and winding, but the devotees patiently waited, adhering to the instructions of the volunteers. Suddenly, there was a small commotion. The volunteers tried to find out the cause of the disturbance, and learned that a man, a local bully known for his waywardness, was intentionally trying to upset the tranquility of the situation. Try as they

1 Crisp, wafer-like Indian chips, typically of circular shape, made from lentil flour.

might, the volunteers could not control this miscreant, who sent ripples of displeasure among the devotees. He continued misbehaving until he reached Amma. She held him for a few seconds more than usual. Her hug had the effect of calming him. When he left, it was as a sober and silent man, such was the transformation of his demeanor. Reports have it that he turned over a new leaf, much to the astonishment of his neighbors and people of his locality.

Amma advises, "The purpose of the human birth is the realization of one's own Self, the result of which is total silence and serenity of the inner instrument." Man is striving for happiness each and every moment but in the wrong direction and in the wrong way. Actually, we are all unknowingly searching for the Self. Seeking happiness and seeking the Self are one and the same thing. The nature of the Self is bliss (happiness). Only one blessed with a competent Guru can realize the Self. One can never be enlightened unless the ego is totally annihilated. To remove the sense of 'I' and 'mine,' the guidance of a true master is indispensable.

Actually, 'I' is never a problem, but 'mine' is always a problem. We tend to attach the sense of 'mine' to everything, and hence suffer. To say, "I am the servant of servants/Amma/God" is very easy. To put it into practice is very difficult. Who is the troublemaker? Is it the mind?

Not really; the mind has no strength of its own. It is inert, but we go on feeding and nourishing it. The mind is like the moon, and the Self, like the sun. The moon can never shine without light from the sun. Likewise, the mind derives energy from the Self. Therefore, we should watch what we feed the inert mind. If we feed it egoic thoughts, it becomes selfish, and if left unchecked, can persist until the end of life. The puffed-up ego is like an extremely adamant child; it never obeys. It becomes master of the real master (the Self). At that stage, the real master cannot control it. One might try to control it, but the mind will say, "I am not prepared to obey you. You have come too late." Indulging in every whim fattens the ego, making the mind a spoilt brat – disobedient and uncontrollable. It becomes the master. The goal of spiritual life is to gain mastery over the mind so that true bliss can be experienced. Obedience to the Master's guidance enables one to gain mastery over the mind.

I am reminded of an anecdote. A householder became a staunch believer of a mahātmā and would often visit the swāmi's āśram. One day, he took his wife, children and mother-in-law to the āśram. There, he began introducing his family members to the swāmi. Holding his son, he said, "Swāmiji, this is my son... no, no, he is *your* son! Whatever is mine is yours. I don't have anything." Next he introduced his daughter: "Master, this is *your* daughter." When he introduced his mother-in-law, he emphatically said, "Swāmiji, this is *your* mother-in-law." Poor Swāmi! Who would have imagined that he would gain a son, daughter and a mother-in-law after becoming a sanyāsī! And then, introducing his wife, the devotee said, "And this is *my* wife."

Some may deny being egoistic. Amma says, "To say that one does not have an ego is the greatest form of egoism." The ego alone claims, "I have no ego." Those who are devoid of the ego can perform wonders in this world, though from their plane of consciousness, there are no wonders. It is only from our level that some things appear to be miraculous. The sun provides light to the entire world. There is nothing great about it from the sun's viewpoint. For us, however, it is unimaginably great. Similarly, Amma gives darśan to thousands. We often wonder how She does it, but for Her, it is simple and natural. The secret is total relaxation, which we have to practice each and every moment. The resolves of a pure, relaxed and balanced mind become fruitful.

A devoted family had been coming to the āśram for 10 years. During one visit, the husband and wife started crying on Amma's lap. When asked why, the husband pointed to his wife and said, "She had chest pain a few days ago. We took her to the hospital, where the doctor said that she has four or five blockages in her arteries, and that a bypass surgery is essential."

Consoling them, Amma said in Her usual fashion, "Don't worry, Amma is with you. Nothing will happen. Amma will make a *sankalpa* (divine resolve)."

The couple went home peacefully. The next day, when the wife went for a check-up, the doctor could not find any blockage at all, much to his amazement. You can very well imagine the relief and happiness of the family. They narrated what had happened to the doctor, who said that he wanted to come and see Amma. This incident highlights the surrender of the couple.

In the *Bhagavad Gītā*, Kṛṣṇa offers a guarantee: "*Yōgakṣēmam vahāmyaham*" ("I reward them with what they do not possess, and safeguard for them what they already have") (9.22). However, there is a caveat, mentioned in the same verse, and it is of utmost significance: "*Ananyāścintayantō mām*" – "To those who worship Me alone, thinking of nothing else." In other words, the Lord should be worshipped with one-pointedness. Amma is very particular about this, too. When She enters the mind, no one else should be there. It should also be devoid of craving for sensual objects.

The ego has usurped the throne that rightfully belongs to inner divinity. Through His crucifixion and resurrection, Jesus was giving out to all of humanity the cardinal message that one should transcend the body and be reborn into the Supreme. The cross looks as if the letter 'I' has been struck out, and the crucifixion stands for the denial of the body, an emblem of the ego.

If we do each and every action without the sense of ego, we will always be peaceful. Goddess Saraswatī is shown seated on a lotus in a lake. How is it that the lotus remains afloat? Does the law of gravity not apply to goddesses? The fact is, the lotus remains afloat because the Goddess does not possess the weight of an ego.

Actually, the ego is an illusion. An example will prove the point. Take the case of an apartment. While staying in it, one feels, "This is my apartment." Suppose one has to shift to a new place. The sense of identification will, in due course, shift to the new home. Needless to say, the apartment has no such feeling. What causes this attachment is *māyā*, the cosmic force of delusion that creates a sense of 'mineness' and makes us bound to the fleeting objects of the world.

A person traveling alone at night saw something, which he imagined to be a ghost, and became frightened. When he mustered enough courage to beam his torchlight on it, he realized that it was only a post. The man saw the ghost in the post only because there was fear in him. If he had been free of fear, there would not have been a misapprehension. Amma is teaching us to calm our minds and thus control ourselves. In order to merge ourselves in the Truth, we must first learn to relax our minds. If we carry a burden of tensions all the time, how can we relax? How can we attain the Truth? Very often, our instincts get in the way of mental peace.

After Rāma killed Rāvaṇa, the Lord returned to Ayōdhyā, where He was duly crowned king. Thereafter, he wanted to arrange a feast for His monkey friends, who had sincerely served Him. Rāma's brother, Lakṣmaṇa, however, had reservations about this. Although he acknowledged the monkeys' sincerity, he did not think too highly of their nature, and felt that it would be very difficult for them to change, even in Ayōdhyā, Rāma's abode. Rāma told him that his doubts were unfounded.

The feast was arranged. All the monkeys came to eat. They were on their best behavior. Everything was peaceful and calm. Lord Rāma was extremely happy. But alas, when buttermilk was being served, one monkey saw a lemon seed in it (lemon juice had been added to it). He instinctively made a grab for it, and the seed slipped through his hand and flew into the air. Seeing this, the monkey jumped to catch it. Seeing him leaping into the air, his simian friends thought it was a game to see who could jump highest. Soon, there was total pandemonium, with leaping monkeys and food all over the place!

It is difficult to refine one's basic nature, but it is not impossible to change. Are not all our pleasures and pains non-existent during deep sleep? It is as though we have forgotten or gone beyond everything. We should try to attain the state of awareness and bliss all the time, following Amma's advice: "O man, arise, awake and dive deep within your Self. Enjoy supreme bliss."

When ordinary people talk or do something thoughtless, the consequences can even disturb the equilibrium of nature. However, when spiritual masters like Amma speak, the positive vibrations of their words become like a divine wish or prayer that reflects and registers everywhere. The whole universe moves to make their words a reality. That this world continues to prevail despite all the atrocities human beings are committing is only because of the presence of divine incarnations like Amma. Avatars are like ballasts in the universe's evolutionary voyage, ensuring that existence maintains an even keel and does not flounder or capsize on account of man's degradation. Masters always pray for the peace and happiness of all beings; they never seek anything for themselves.

Amma says, "Children, you need to have the certificate of even an ant in order to achieve success in your sādhana." Her deference to nature speaks volumes about Her oneness with nature.

Years ago, when I was in yellow robes (Br. Praṇavāmṛta Caitanya) and had been entrusted with looking after the branch āśram in Tiruvanantapuram, every trip back to Amṛtapuri was fraught with the anticipation of seeing Amma. As soon as I arrived, I would somehow try to get Amma's attention. Often, I would stand below Amma's room and start belting out devotional songs for Her to hear. For some reason, I was never self-conscious; it did not even strike me to wonder what others might think of me as I stood there, looking up at Amma's room and singing loudly. I was quite focused on my objective: meeting Amma. As far as I was concerned, I was serenading my Beloved Mother. Sometimes, I would even cough loudly to get Her attention. Usually, She would send someone soon to call me into Her room. Not only that, She was so sensitive that She would be able to gauge my state of mind from my voice. For example, She would say things like, "From your cough, I can tell that you are stressed about something. What is it?"

Once, though, none of my strategies worked. I sang and sang, and coughed and coughed, all in vain! When I was tiring and about to admit defeat, I saw a curious sight. A crow flew to the window of Amma's room and perched on something. When I looked, I saw that it was Amma's hand. There were peanuts in one hand, and the crow was using its beak to pick up individual nuts. When I peered more closely into the window, I saw Amma using Her other hand to pick up some of the peanuts and throw them swiftly into Her mouth. As far as I knew, crows never go too close to human beings, but this one was literally eating out of Her hands. Without waiting for an invitation, I took the liberty of going into Amma's room.

As soon as I entered, Amma called out, "Praṇavam!" without turning around to look. When I went near Amma, the crow instinctively moved away.

I asked Amma, "How is it that the crow was fearlessly sitting on Your hand? Isn't that unusual?"

"No, son," Amma replied, "Birds and beasts have always been my friends. They used to feed me during the days of my sādhana. I don't see the crow as different from me."

Though spoken with natural simplicity, Amma's words struck me as giving a glimpse into Her sublime spiritual stature. A Self-realized soul beholds the one Self in all beings, and this realization manifests itself as exceptional kinship with all beings. Even animals and birds can sense the vibrations of love and non-violence emanating from

Amma. That was why the crow had fearlessly perched on Her hand.

I then asked, "Amma, who is that crow?" I wanted to know if it was some special being.

Amma shrugged Her shoulders, feigning ignorance. I persisted. After a while, She said, "He is a departed soul. He used to be a human being. Now, perhaps owing to past association with Amma, he feels a spontaneous attraction towards me."

I noticed that Amma used the pronoun for human beings ('he'), not 'it.' Clearly, She saw through the form that clothed this soul. I then asked Her, "If someone is Your devotee in this life, is that person likely to be reborn as a crow?"

Amma brushed aside my inquiry. "Why worry about this, son? What matters is what you do in this life, how you use it to advance towards the goal of the human birth."

I felt that Amma was reminding me of the singularly good fortune of having come under Her divine tutelage. Not just me, millions of people all over the world have been thus blessed. What matters is whether we make full use of the opportunity of having met a mahātmā like Amma to inspire progress on the pilgrimage to divinity.

I was reminded of what Lord Kṛṣṇa said in the *Bhagavad Gītā*:

ābrahmabhuvanāllokāḥ punarāvartinōSrjuna
māmupētya tu kauntēya punarjanma na vidyatē
All the worlds, O Arjuna, including the realm of Brahmā, are subject to return.
But after attaining Me, O son of Kuntī, there is no rebirth. (8.16)

These words sound daunting, because they indicate that even *Brahma-lōka*, the world of Brahmā, the Creator, is not the highest realm. Lofty though that world is, one who attains it must, upon completion of the *kalpa* (about 4.32 billion years),[2] be reborn again. Only one who has transcended the cycle of birth and death can merge in the Supreme, which Lord Kṛṣṇa embodies. We are blessed to have with us another such incarnation. May this sacred verse inspire us to attain Amma, the very personification of divinity.

There is an intelligent way of classifying people: 1. those who arrive, live and depart in ignorance; 2. those who come in ignorance, acquire knowledge through spiritual life, and depart in knowledge; and 3. those who are born, live in and depart in full knowledge. The rare few, like

2 Or one whole day of Lord Brahmā, the Creator in the Hindu Trinity. One kalpa is made up of 1,000 *mahāyugas*; one mahāyuga is made up of four *yugas* (see Glossary). It spans the period from creation to dissolution of the universe.

Amma, fall into the last category. Most fall into the first category. We ought at least to aspire and strive earnestly to gain membership in the second category.

Our ignorance is often odd and amusing. A mother wrote the following letter to her son:

> My dear son,
>
> I'm writing this letter slowly because I know you cannot read fast. The weather here isn't too bad. It rained only twice this week: the first time, it rained for three days, and the second time, for four days. You wanted me to send you your jacket, but your aunt said it would be a little too heavy to send the jacket with all its metal buttons by post. So we cut them off and put them in the pocket. Your father has a new job, with 500 men under him. He cuts grass at the cemetery. Your sister had a baby this morning. I haven't found out whether it's a girl or a boy. So, I don't know whether you are an aunt or uncle.
>
> Your Uncle Jeff fell into a liquor barrel. Some men tried to pull him out, but he fought them off bravely and drowned. We cremated him and he burned for three days. Your best friend, Tom, is no more. He died trying to fulfill his father's last wish, which was to be buried in the sea after he died. Tom died

while digging a grave for his father. Nothing else has happened.

Love,

Mom

P.S. I was going to send you some money but by the time I remembered it, the envelope was already sealed.

There is a humorous anecdote on the gross ignorance of students and teachers from a certain school. The great epic, *Rāmāyaṇa*, was part of the curriculum, and the segment being taught was about how King Janaka had in his possession the *tryambaka*, a mighty bow that belonged to Lord Śiva. The king had decided to offer his daughter's hand in marriage to one who could successfully lift and string the great bow.

The teacher was, however, not very interested in the subject, and was sitting in his chair, enjoying a siesta, much to his students' delight. They formed groups and started enacting war games using projectiles made from pencils, paper balls and other objects. The classroom was a picture of total chaos. Some children were pulling each other's hair. A few were decorating the blackboard with works of art. Yet others were simulating cricket moves and karate chops. Just then, one of the inspectors from the state department of education walked in for an inspection. Shocked by the classroom anarchy, he walked up to the sleeping teacher and, slamming his hand on the desk, demanded, "What's going on here?"

The teacher sprung up from his chair and, grabbing the textbook, explained, "I was just teaching them the story from the *Rāmāyaṇa* about the tryambaka bow and who broke it."

The inspector said, "Oh really? Then let us see how much your students have grasped!" Pointing his finger at one of the boys, the inspector asked, "Tell me, who broke the tryambaka?"

Trembling, the boy stuttered, "It... it... it wasn't me, sir, I promise you! Honestly, I didn't do it!"

The inspector then turned to the class bully and asked him, "Young man, maybe you can tell me who broke the bow."

The boy glared at the inspector and said, "Don't you dare threaten me like that! I don't care who you are, even if you are an inspector. Don't mess with me!"

The inspector became furious and asked a third boy, who pointed at the girl next to him and said, "It was her. I saw her do it!"

Outraged by the children's responses, he asked the teacher, "What have you been teaching here? What kind of school is this? How do you explain this?"

The teacher replied in a pleading tone, "Honestly, sir, these children might seem mischievous but they would *never* break that bow! I trust them fully. Please believe me."

The inspector felt ridiculed and went to see the principal. Entering the principal's office, he asked, "What kind of school are you running? I came on an inspection to ensure that the children are being taught their lessons well. When I asked a simple question – 'Who broke the tryambaka?' – none of them could answer. Shockingly, even the class teacher was ignorant! How do you expect me to let your school pass this inspection?"

The response from the principal was even more outrageous. He vehemently exclaimed, "How dare you accuse the children of my school! They would *never* break Rāma's bow. They are not so destructive."

This story might sound far-fetched but it illustrates how we prove to be ignorant of the Self when the moment of divine inspection arrives. What's worse is that many of us are ignorant of our ignorance! How can we eradicate this ignorance? By surrendering before a true master, like Amma.

The ways of the Master can sometimes seem strange and bewildering. I recall an incident that happened several years ago. It was the eve of my ceremonial initiation into *sanyāsa*, the final vow of renunciation. The other brahmacārīs and I who were being initiated were fasting and observing a vow of silence, as instructed by Amma. Day became night as we continued to prepare ourselves mentally for this sacred occasion. As the night progressed, I remained awake. Thoughts of being ushered into the path of sanyāsa, the ceremonial procedures involved, and the responsibilities that came with it were uppermost in my mind.

At about 12:30 a.m., someone knocked on my door. When I opened the door, the person standing outside said, "Quick, Amma is calling you!" I was surprised. Why would She call me at that hour, I wondered? Perhaps, Amma wanted to impart some last-minute instruction to enlighten me on certain aspects of the path I was about to enter. Maybe, She wanted to introduce me to distinguished visitors who had come to the āśram on the eve of this solemn occasion.

I hurriedly went to Amma's room and knocked on the door. There was no one there. So, I went in search of Her. Soon, I learned that She had gone to another part of the āśram, where 'Operation Clean Septic Tank' was underway! As I approached the site, I heard Amma's voice. I closed my eyes, thinking that I was hearing Her voice from my inner senses, but it was not so. I was now very close to the septic tank. When I looked in, I saw Amma standing inside, looking up and smiling sweetly at me.

There were a few others inside the tank with Amma – no distinguished guests there! Amma said, "Oh, there you are! I was looking for you. Now, come and help me!"

Amma was cleaning the septic tank, which was filled and was almost overflowing, spreading a foul smell. Though I had done similar sēva in the past, I never thought I would have to do it again. I was thoroughly repulsed by the sight and foul smell, but there was no escape. I slowly and squeamishly made my way down into the septic tank to join Amma, who immediately handed me a bucket and started filling it with excreta. As I was holding the full bucket and wondering what to do with it, Amma looked at me and asked why I was not passing it to the person outside the septic tank. The bucket was dripping wet. How was I going to lift it above my head and pass it to the person outside without spilling its repulsive contents on my head? I even considered returning the bucket to Amma. However, with Her grace, I thought better and passed the bucket. As the work progressed and the septic tank became cleaner, I noticed that my burden was becoming lighter. Finally, the job was done.

Although I was not introduced to any distinguished guest, I was conscious of the overwhelming proximity of Amma, the distinguished master. I had been blessed with the singularly great fortune of being led and blessed by

Amma on the eve of this important milestone of my life. Heaven only knows the happiness and elation I derived that night.

Lord Kṛṣṇa says,

> *yattadagrē viṣamiva pariṇāmēऽmṛtōpamam*
> *tatsukham sāttvikam prōktamātmabuddhiprasādajam*
> That which is like poison at first, but like nectar at the end;
> that happiness is declared to be sattwic, born of the translucence of intellect due to Self-realization.
> (*Bhagavad* Gītā, 18.37)

Amma has said, "A spiritual seeker should perform every action with equanimity of mind, rising above personal preference. You love and care for a charming, good-looking child but you feel aversion towards an ugly-looking child born into a low caste. These distinctions are common among worldly people, who dwell in the world of likes and dislikes. Remember that the sole purpose of your life is to transcend these distinctions, all likes and dislikes."

Once, when Rāma and Sītā were in exile in the forest, Sītā spotted an emerald-green parrot of exquisite beauty. Perhaps, intuiting His divinity, the parrot became a ready captive to Rāma. He handed it over to Sītā, who beamed with joy at this prize catch. She gazed wonderstruck at the parrot's variegated beauty, and then asked Her Lord what they should name it. After a moment's thought, Rāma said, "Kaikēyī."

Rāma's stepmother, Kaikēyī, had been the driving force in ensuring that He was banished from Ayōdhyā. She had obstinately insisted that Daśaratha bequeath the throne of the lunar dynasty to her son, Bharata, and not to Rāma, who was the heir and eldest son. In spite of all the hardships that He had had to bear as a result of Kaikēyī's vicious willfulness and animosity towards Him, Rāma did not bear the slightest grudge towards her. When her decision had been made known to Him on the eve of His coronation, Rāma had accepted it with utmost equanimity. He truly saw the divine hand in every dispensation. That He could think of Kaikēyī, the architect of his trials and tribulations, in association with exceptional beauty, and that, too, when He was not in the public gaze and could, therefore, be said to have His guard down, attests very clearly to how He never fell under the sway of likes and dislikes. His love was divine, i.e. without any polar opposite.

May each one of us be like a grain of sand, prepared to accept silently every footfall with a smile, like a humble servant. Mother Earth accepts everything with patience. Such ought to be the attitude of a person who desires to realize God.

5
"Who's that lady standing under the tree?"

O Lord, give me sorrows and sufferings! Only then can I remember You always."

Not many people can pray like this. It takes maturity, wisdom and immense fortitude to see the silver lining of spiritual opportunity behind the dark clouds of suffering. This fervent prayer arose from the heart of Kuntī, mother of the Pāṇḍavas. She recognized that problems were inevitable in life, and that they could kindle the flame of devotion in human hearts. This was not mere doctrine for her; it was borne out by personal experience.

The Pāṇḍavas had been subjected to a long series of trials and tribulations that culminated in the Mahābhārata War, and Lord Kṛṣṇa had been their loyal companion during all their struggles. During the *Rājasūya Yajña*, He had washed the feet of the invited guests and cleared the leftovers from their discarded food leaves. When Duśśāsana had, at Duryōdhana's instigation, publicly humiliated Pāñcālī, the wife of the Pāṇḍavas, Kṛṣṇa had protected her modesty. Kṛṣṇa had been by the side of the Pāṇḍavas during their 12-year forest domicile and the one year they had to remain incognito. As soon as they had vanquished all their enemies and regained the kingdom, which was rightfully theirs, Kṛṣṇa had left for Dvāraka. For Mother Kuntī, His departure symbolized an important lesson: that God is closer to His devotees in times of need and distress;

hence, her ardent supplication to Lord Kṛṣṇa for the boon of sorrow and suffering.

Given the inevitability of problems, one should not waste time asking, "Why is this happening to me?" By allowing ourselves to become overwhelmed by a problem, we create unnecessary suffering for ourselves. We think that nothing is more important than our troubles. Instead of tackling them intelligently, we attach undue significance to trivialities, thus making mountains out of molehills. This approach is like giving milk to a snake; sooner or later, it will bite us. Instead of empowering the problem, we ought to neutralize its charge.

A problem is like an onion. When we start to peel one layer after another, we find that there is nothing left of the onion at the end. Similarly, if we analyze any problem in life with a clear head, we will soon find nothing left of the problem. In other words, where there is a problem, there is always a solution. We just have to approach the situation with the right attitude. Fretting over problems is like sitting on a rocking chair – it moves a lot but goes nowhere!

In 1995, Amma asked me to take charge of the Mumbai āśram. After four years, the hectic schedule of programs began to affect my health. I started suffering from various ailments. More than anything else, I was mentally fatigued. I wanted to return to Kēraḷa, and asked Amma if I could.

She said no, even though I pleaded with Her repeatedly. After a while, in response to my continuing entreaties, all that She would say was, "Amma will let you know." I felt defeated and dejected.

One day, while looking down from my room in the Mumbai āśram, I saw a brahmacārī performing *ārati* in the Brahmasthānam temple. Somehow, the sight of the burning camphor tablets being reduced to nothing moved me to compose a bhajan. The result was *'Karppūradīpam.'*

karppūradīpam tozhutu nilkkumbōḷ
uḷḷattileṅgō ñān mōhiccu:
ammē, dēvī, amṛtavarṣiṇi,
karppūramāyirunnenkil, ñānā
karppūramāyirunnenkil!

While standing prayerfully before the burning camphor lamp, a desire arose from somewhere deep inside me. O Mother, O Goddess, who showers the nectar of immortality, if only I were that camphor, if only I were that camphor!

sādhakanallivan ammē, janma –
vēdanayenne grasippū.
nīrum manassinnorāśvāsam ēkuvān
tūmandahāsam pozhikkū, māyē,
tūmandahāsam pozhikkū!

O Mother, I am no spiritual aspirant. The pains of life ensnare me. O Goddess of Illusion, beam Your graceful smile so that my smoldering mind can enjoy some solace, beam Your graceful smile!

bhōgāśayērunnu nīḷē – pinne
tyāgāśayētumēyilla.
kālam vṛthāvilāvunnu dayāmayī,
cārattaṇayāttatentē, dēvī,
cārattaṇayāttatentē?
The desire for enjoyment continues to arise incessantly, smothering the desire for renunciation. Time is running out, O Compassionate One. Why don't You come to me, O Goddess, why don't You come to me?

In those days, I could visit Amṛtapuri only once every three or four months. After I had finished composing the bhajan, I recorded it during my next visit to Amṛtapuri. Once again, I pleaded with Amma to consider my request to return to Kērala but received no positive response. I went back to Mumbai, feeling more dejected than ever before.

One day, while chanting the *Laḷitā Aṣṭōttaram* (108 attributes of the Divine Mother) in the Mumbai āśram, I was struck anew by one of the mantras:

om candraśēkhara bhaktārthi bhañjanāyai namō namaḥ
Salutations to the Divine Mother, who removes the distress of devotees who worship Lord Śiva. (77)

Śakti, the principle of pure energy, is not separate from Śiva, the principle of pure consciousness. Therefore, one who worships Śiva also pleases Śakti, personified as the Divine Mother. The only way in which I could move Amma with my plight was by appeasing Her. I decided that I would do so by worshipping Lord Śiva!

For the next 41 days, I personally performed the pūja in the Brahmasthānam Temple, much to the surprise of devotees, who wondered why I was secluding myself in the sanctum sanctorum for hours together. I also fasted frequently during this period. I never let anyone in on the reason; it was a sacred tryst between me and the Divine Mother. As I sat in the shrine, I would first chant the 108 attributes of Amma. I would then chant sacred verses to invoke Lord Śiva's grace and pray sincerely with devotion. Finally, I would also chant the 108 attributes of Lord Śiva accompanied by the offering of 108 three-clove *bilva* leaves (considered dear to Lord Śiva) duly dipped in water mixed with red sandalwood powder. I prayed with all my heart and soul, and concluded the 41-day worship.

A day or two later, my telephone rang at about midnight. It was Amma. She said, "Son, I was listening to the recording of '*Karppūradīpam*' and thought of you. That's why I called." Amma's voice was full of love and compassion. Some instinct told me that if I presented my case right now, She would relent.

I asked, "Amma, can I tell you something?"

"What is it, my son?" Amma asked, Her voice full of motherly compassion.

I then opened up my heart and told Her how I was unhappy in the Mumbai āśram and about the illnesses I was suffering without respite. I pleaded with Her to let me return to Kēraḷa. Amma said, "Alright, son, come back and take charge of the Pālakkāṭ and Triśśūr āśrams."

In hindsight, I feel that it was purely divine grace that opened my eyes to a 'strategy' to melt the Divine Mother's heart, thus paving the way for my return to Kēraḷa. Although I found it difficult to stay away from Amma's physical presence, I obeyed Her instructions to stay put in Mumbai. Nevertheless, I devoted time and energy to praying fervently. I believe that the sincerity of my prayers moved Amma's heart, and thus helped me secure a transfer from Mumbai.

In the previous chapter, it was noted that the mind in itself is inert, but we feel confounded by the tangled knot of thoughts and misconceptions we feed it. The *Yōga Vāsiṣṭha* wryly notes, "One who says that he was destroyed by the mind, which has no substantiality at all, says in effect that his head was smashed by a lotus petal. To say that one can be hurt by the mind – which is inert, dumb and blind – is like saying that one was roasted by the heat of the full moon."

There was a man who was fond of teaching his dog novel tricks. One day, he thought of teaching it the English alphabet and then a few words that could be strung together to form simple sentences. He succeeded considerably. One day, when the dog was taken out for a walk, it saw a sign on the gate of a private house. The dog enthusiastically ran to the gate and, using its forelegs, raised itself to read the sign. The owner looked on in awe, until he saw the hangdog expression on his pet's face. Within seconds, teardrops were flowing from its eyes. That is when the owner noticed the sign: "Dogs Not Allowed."

Like the man's educational plans for his canine, our misbegotten initiatives often cause problems. The other mistake that creates unnecessary suffering is giving undue importance to the opinions of others. Amma says, "Our minds should not be controlled by the tongues of others. Complaining that people find fault with us is akin to whining about a mosquito bite. That is the nature of mosquitoes. If one has the right understanding, one will never bother about the misunderstandings of others."

Once, while an Indian prince was traveling by ship, he fell overboard accidentally. An Irish passenger rescued him. The prince, who was abundantly rich, offered to reward the Irish man for saving his life. The savior declined, but when the Indian prince persisted, the Irishman said, "Alright. When you visit Dublin, you can get me a few golf clubs."

A few months later, they met in Dublin. The prince apologetically said, "I'm sorry. You must think me very ungrateful. But I'm having trouble buying you golf clubs. I could not buy the Portmarnock Golf Club for love or money. I am now trying to buy Dollymount, Hermitage and one or two other clubs. In the meantime, I have purchased 150 acres of land. As soon as the legal procedures are completed, I will see to it that the course is laid out in haste."

Such misunderstandings are legion. When asked about a misunderstanding, a simpleton thought that the speaker was referring to a young lady (Miss) standing under (understanding) a tree, and wanted to know who she was! Whoever she may be, leave her alone! If we do not bother too much with misunderstandings, they, too, will leave us alone.

An oft-repeated story is of a venerated saint who lived alone in his monastery. He was known for his spotless spiritual virtues, and his sterling reputation spread far and wide. There was a young, beautiful maiden staying in the neighborhood. One day, the locality woke up to the shocking news that she was pregnant. Her angry father wanted to know who was responsible for the pregnancy. When he questioned her, she pointed to the saint.

The aspersion cast on the sage ruined his reputation. He was subjected to a great deal of ridicule and humiliation. However, he remained untouched by the insinuations and vibes of the people around.

After the maiden had given birth, the father took the baby to the sage, saying, "Here's the result of your misdeeds!"

The saint merely said, "Is that so?"

Two years passed. Unable to bear her guilt any longer, the unwed mother confessed that the father of her illegitimate child was not the saint but one of the prominent men of the locality. The people were filled with remorse for having behaved in the most unbecoming manner. Representatives of the locality accompanied the unwed mother and her father to the saint and begged for forgiveness. They requested him to hand over the child to them. Once again, the sage's response was laconic: "Oh! Is that so?"

In both situations – the first in which people were menacing and antagonistic, and the second in which the same people were contrite and submissive – the sage remained even-minded. Such is the mental equilibrium that one must achieve if one wishes to progress spiritually. A seeker must constantly strive to attain this state of equanimity.

Life reflects the constant conflict between good and bad. However, no matter how strong the evil may be, truth will prevail in the end. Ultimately, might is not always right; it is right that has might. There are innumerable examples from the *Purāṇas* that illustrate this law. For instance, Duryōdhana had seemingly everything on his side – the largest army, as well as invincible and experienced campaigners like Bhīṣma, Drōṇa and Karṇa – all of which pointed to a certain victory for him. But he was vanquished by a modest army led by men of moral substance. Why did this happen? '*Satyamēva jayatē*' – 'Truth alone triumphs' is an unequivocally proclaimed Upaniṣadic statement. This universal law will always be upheld, no matter how the tides may seem to flow. The clouds may obscure the sun but this does not negate its existence. The clouds can only prevent us from seeing the sun temporarily. In the *Mahābhārata*, we see that Duryōdhana was swayed by *adharma* (unrighteousness) and divorced from all truth.

It was only a matter of time before the winds of *dharma* (righteousness) blew away the dark clouds of adharma to reveal the sun of Truth.

Many devotees of Amma were understandably shocked and distressed by the recent spate of allegations that a former āśram resident made against Her and some of the āśram's senior sanyāsīs. Devotees from all over the world rallied around Mother, defending Her, the monks and the āśram. Amidst the clamorous protests voiced by these well-wishers, Amma's gentle and loving voice of wisdom was almost drowned out. Referring to Herself and the āśram's activities as an open book, Amma then pointed out how mahātmās have been wrongly slandered and persecuted since time immemorial. Asking Her children to refrain from indulging in crude mob behavior, Amma encouraged them to be patient, saying that the truth will be revealed sooner or later. It seems Her preferred response to such situations is dignified silence, which She displayed even at the time of Her birth.

Once, Emperor Akbar drew a line and asked his wise minister Bīrbal to shorten the line without cutting or erasing it in any way. Bīrbal merely drew a longer line next to Akbar's line. Similarly, the noble arch and trajectory of Amma's life will undoubtedly prove the lines that Her detractors have been spewing to be short on truth.

Actually, the recent smear campaign was not the first that has been directed against Amma. She has been repeatedly slandered, but She has taken them in Her stride with forbearance, forgiving Her detractors unconditionally.

Lord Kṛṣṇa was also often misunderstood by many during His time and was the subject of much censure. When He advised Satrājit, who had obtained the Syamantaka gem from the Sun-god, to give the gem to King Ugrasēna, Satrājit refused, saying that the gem was rightfully his. Kṛṣṇa's only interest was the welfare of the people. He knew that the Syamantaka would yield an enormous amount of gold every morning, which the king could use for the welfare of his subjects. If it remained in Satrājit's hands alone, he would hoard all the wealth for himself. The advice was ignored. A chain of events led to the death of Prasēna, Satrājit's brother, who was then holding on to the Syamantaka. Satrājit accused Kṛṣṇa of killing his brother to gain the Syamantaka. Although Kṛṣṇa's innocence was eventually proved, never once did He protest when accused. Like the sage falsely accused of fathering a child, Kṛṣṇa's equanimity was unwavering.

In the Trētā Yuga, Lord Rāma did not react when He heard on the eve of His coronation that He was to be banished to the forest. In the Dvāpara Yuga, Kṛṣṇa was accused of everything, from being a thief to a philanderer.

In the Kali Yuga, Amma and other mahātmās have similarly been charged with crimes they never committed. History has clearly shown that greatness attracts not just bouquets but brickbats as well. What is interesting is the characteristic response of mahātmās to both: utter detachment.

One may even go so far as to say that mahātmās invite censure to show human beings how one should respond in such situations—with love and equanimity. Quite possibly, even the divine incarnations who have graced the earth with their sanctifying presence have, without exception, been subject to stinging criticism. This cannot be attributed to the law of karma, because even their birth was not the fruit of actions done in the past, unlike ours. Just as they chose to be born on earth in order to elevate humankind to Godhood, they have chosen to be willing subjects to the basest potshots that humanity is capable of hurling, if only to absorb the poison that would otherwise destroy the world.

This is exactly what Lord Śiva did: he swallowed the lethal poison that emerged from the mouth of the serpent Vāsuki when the gods and demons churned the ocean of milk in order to gain the nectar of immortality. Unlike most of us who yearn for fame, the great Gurus, the humble servants of humanity, do not seek the limelight. When faced with infamy, their unimpeachable conduct eventually proves their righteousness. Calculated attempts to tarnish their holy name ultimately serve to reveal their unblemished nature.

Amma once told me, "At a time when the whole world mocked and accused me, I laughed in amusement at the detractors because I knew that my real state was one of pure bliss."

On another occasion, She said, "People might glorify or slander us at any time without any reason. This is the nature of the world. But a knower of Truth accepts both with even-mindedness."

All that come and go are transient. For those who have transcended the empirical level, which is what we are familiar with, worldly life takes on the quality of a surreal dream. In fact, for God-realized souls, the world is an illusion, pure hallucination, as the following story from the *Yōga Vāsiṣṭha* shows:

> There once lived three princes who hailed from a city that did not exist. Two of these princes were not born, and the third had not been conceived. Fate was not too kind on them, for all their near and dear ones died. Unable to bear the sorrow, the princes left home. They trudged on without knowing where they were going. The scorching heat of the midsummer sun overhead, the hot sand

beneath their feet, and the hot blasts of air all around conspired to make them exhausted. They somehow crawled towards the shade of three trees, two of which were non-existent; the third had yet to be planted. They ate fruits from the trees to appease their hunger, after which they rested in the cool shade.

Towards evening, they left and continued walking until they reached the banks of three rivers. Two were dried up and the third was without water. The three princes quenched their thirst by drinking the water, after which they enjoyed a cool bath. They then continued walking until they reached a mega-city that had not been constructed yet. Here, they saw three palaces of unmatched splendor. Two of these palaces had not been built yet, whereas the third did not even have walls. Walking into the palaces, the princes saw three golden plates, two broken into pieces and the third smashed to smithereens. Taking the last plate, the princes filled it with 99 minus 100 grams of rice, which they then cooked. After that, they invited three *sādhus* to join them for their evening repast. Of the three, two had no body, and the third, no mouth. After these holy men had eaten, the three princes ate the remaining rice. How pleased they were! In this way, they continued living in this mega-city for a long time, happy and contented.

A mind established in God is free from delusion and unaffected by good or bad. It is the sense of duality that causes agitation of the mind. The conviction that there is only either pleasure or pain is attributable to the intellect, but there is a state of joy that transcends these dualities. One must go beyond the intellect to attain that state. To quote Robert Louis Stevenson, "Quiet minds cannot be perplexed or frightened, but go on in fortune or misfortune at their own private pace, like a clock during a thunderstorm."

6
"What happened to your tapas?"

Tradition holds that when one goes on a pilgrimage to Kāśī (Vārāṇasī), one should give up a desire. Some people give up coffee or tea, which they could not do without until then. The point behind this belief is that it weakens the stranglehold that desires have on us. Only when we give up our likes and dislikes can the divine will flow through us unobstructed, thus paving the way for our own spiritual liberation.

A person who recently went on a pilgrimage to Kāśī told me that after he returned, he gave up bitter gourd. He did not like it anyway, so it was not much of a sacrifice! This is a travesty of a hallowed tradition.

Such is the condition of the world today. There is little truth or goodness. Everything is adulterated; nothing is genuine. We give undue importance to labels. The following story illustrates this point.

There was once a sincere seeker doing penance under a banyan tree. A group of black monkeys (*karinkurangu*) sitting in the tree kept disturbing him. The ascetic stoically bore everything. Finally, a naughty monkey urinated on him. Enraged, the ascetic thundered, "May you all be made into *Karinkurangu Rasāyanam*[3] in the Kali Yuga!"

---

3 An ancient Āyurvēdic medicine prepared in dire emergencies from parts of a black monkey's body.

When they heard these words, the monkeys became frightened. They realized that the ascetic's curse would bear fruit. Feeling bewildered and helpless, they went to see their chief, Hanumān. "O Lord, please protect us," they beseeched. "In our foolishness and ignorance, we hurt a great ascetic and incurred his wrath. He damned us all, saying that we would be used as ingredients for some medicine (*rasāyanam*) in the Kali Yuga. What will happen to our race? Please protect us!"

Lord Hanumān approached the ascetic to plead on behalf of the naughty monkeys. "O Master, please spare them. Let not the race of monkeys be destroyed. Kindly forgive them their mistakes."

Moved by Hanumān's entreaties, the sage agreed to soften the curse. He said, "The medicine will only carry the 'Karinkurangu Rasāyanam' label. It won't have anything to do with monkeys."

The monkeys retreated, highly relieved.

This may only be a story, but it reflects the state of affairs today. Nothing is genuine; everything is merely covered by a veneer of truth or genuineness. A few years ago, there was a newspaper report about a reputed medical practitioner who would, while pursuing his private practice, insist that patients consulting him pay a hefty fee, although he was very rich. Moreover, this doctor would unnecessarily refer many patients for expensive radiological investigations, irrespective of the nature of their illness. To verify this rumor, a journalist went to see this doctor, pretending to be suffering from a headache. The doctor at once referred him for a brain CT scan, without properly assessing his condition. This journalist's subsequent exposé garnered considerable public interest, and the doctor's reputation was ruined. Such black sheep can tarnish the noble name of even good physicians.

Instead of railing against the darkness, Amma prefers that we become sparks of light. Her practice of genuine love, compassion and selflessness glows like a bright spot in this dark age of apathy and self-centeredness. Like Her illumined predecessors, She beholds the oneness behind diversity. The ancient sages declared, "*Ēkam sat*" ("Truth is One") and "*Sarvamidam aham ca brahmaiva*" ("This entire universe and I are verily Brahman"). Those who have been blessed with the transcendental experience of '*Ātmabuddhi-prakāśa*,' the Light that illumines the intellect, act for the welfare of all beings, seeing in everything their own Self.

Amma once remarked, "All forms of spiritual practices are aimed at molding character. If one does not gain mental purity, then what is the use of all these practices?"

Being with Amma is always a soulful experience. Transformation of character and evolution to higher levels of understanding are the hallmarks of spiritual growth. Amma always reminds us, "One should strive to cultivate good habits. Only with the inculcation of good habits can one overcome the bad ones." There is an old adage – "If bad manners are infectious, so are good habits." This shows that the mind is like fertile soil; both the desired plant and the weed can thrive in it. Like a good gardener, we should tend our minds, taking pains to cultivate and nourish good habits, and weed out the bad ones. To quote Eknath Easwaran, philosopher and writer, "Transforming character, conduct and consciousness is not a moral problem. It is an engineering problem." The significance of transforming the mind cannot be understated. As Śrī Rāmakṛṣṇa Paramahamsa said, "It is the mind that makes one wise or ignorant, bound or emancipated."

Amma's advice is sound and practical. For example, She tells children, 1. "Get up early in the morning;" 2. "Obey your parents;" and 3. "Eat only as much as you need." How simple and yet how practical Her advice is! Cultivating moderate eating habits, for example, is not just about how much one should consume, but also about using one's physical and intellectual faculties to exercise restraint and to temper the mind's excesses, thus enabling spiritual progress. Montesquieu, the French writer and philosopher, alluded to the importance of eating in moderation when he quipped, "Lunch kills half of Paris, supper the other half."

Cultivating good habits and eradicating bad ones purify the mind, and thus pave the way to spiritual liberation. Amma says, "Eventually, one should aim to transcend both good and bad tendencies. In the ultimate analysis, the absolute truth is beyond both."

In the early days, Amma would take Her children to Kaṇvāśram, a vast estate of pristine land with hillocks, trees, streams and ponds, where a maharṣi named Kaṇva is believed to have performed intense spiritual austerities. One of the most scenic spots here is a banyan tree, beside which is the Viṣṇu Tīrtham, a sacred pond, which has never dried up, even in the hottest summers. Often, Amma would choose a spot by the pond to meditate, and we would cluster around Her, like bees seeking the nectar of spiritual sweetness. I felt especially inspired by the pilgrimage, and strove to immerse myself fully in penance. I would wake up early and, in pitch darkness, walk to the pond, unmindful of snakes and other creatures. I would then sit for hours in meditation. When I was not meditating, I would either walk around, chanting my mantra, or read from the *Bhāgavatam*.

Often, I used to stay alone in Kaṇvāśram for meditation. For me, the *Bhāgavatam* was more than just a font of religious inspiration; it was literally a pillar of support—whenever I was frightened at night, I would clutch this book and try to sleep! When I recounted this to Amma, She would roar with laughter and, for many years, would often mention this story whenever She spoke about my 'valor.'

One evening at Kaṇvāśram, Amma narrated the story of Śuka. He was the son of Sage Vyāsa, the illustrious compiler of the Vēdas, and author of the *Purāṇas, Brahmasūtras, Mahābhārata* and the *Śrīmad Bhāgavatam.* The son surpassed the father in spiritual attainment. So complete was his sense of renunciation and so absent his body-consciousness that he left home empty-handed and stark naked. When he walked past a river where celestial nymphs were bathing, they did not cover themselves because they sensed his innate purity, but as soon as Vyāsa appeared, they shyly covered themselves. Looking at us, Amma asked, "Who can walk and act like Śuka?"

I was extremely inspired by Śuka's dispassion. Determined to overcome my sense of body-consciousness and to cultivate dispassion, I shed all my clothes... except my loincloth! I thus shamelessly roamed the grounds of the āśram. Of course, the only reason why I dared to do so was because there was hardly a soul there, save Amma and Her children. I paraded before Amma and the others, and even told Her naïvely, "Amma, You can look if you want! I don't mind!" Amma collapsed in laughter, even as others hooted. But such was my high-minded seriousness that I was not aware of how comic my childish behavior was.

After a few days, when Amma and Her children were about to return to Amṛtapuri, I made an impulsive decision not to leave, but to stay put and dedicate myself to arduous tapas. I announced my decision to Amma: "I will not be returning with You now. I shall return only after 41 days of tapas!"

Amma tried to dissuade me. "Son, once you have come under the guidance of a Guru, it is the Master who decides the path of the disciple. It is not for the disciple to decide what he wants to do."

I did not yield. Without further delay, I shaved my head in preparation for the 'severe austerities.' Seeing no other choice, Amma decided to leave with everyone else. As the hour of Her departure drew close, I broke down crying. Amma simply planted a beautiful kiss on my bald head and walked away. As soon as everyone had left, the significance of my decision struck me. Kaṇvāśram looked desolate! I could not imagine spending even an evening alone, let alone 41 days! Forget tapas! As far as I could see, there was no point living without Amma. Somehow, I pulled through the night. The very next morning, I started walking back from Varkala to Amṛtapuri, a distance of about 68 kilometers! (I did not have any money to take a bus.) With my bald head and ash-smeared face, I must have looked a sight to passers-by!

That evening, after a 12-hour walk, I finally reached Amṛtapuri, home sweet home! It seems that Amma had already told everyone there that I would arrive at any moment. And so, when they sighted me, everyone started laughing. I went straight to Amma and fell at Her feet. "Son, what happened to your tapas?" When I looked up, I saw that Her face was lit by both amusement and infinite compassion. I did not say anything. I had learned my lesson. I knew that I could not bear to stay away from Amma, even for a moment. She was the inspiration and strength behind whatever austerity I could perform. She was also the soul of my life. Without Her, nothing would have any meaning.

In India, utmost importance is attached to '*samskāra*.' The term refers to the totality of one's personality traits that one has acquired as a result of conditioning over many lifetimes. This can also be taken to mean one's level of inner refinement or character. Cultivating an ideal samskāra is central to building the personality of children. If the foundation is well-laid, the child grows steadily, retaining the nucleus of his inner samskāra, even in the face of challenges. It has been observed that the noble samskāra of a person can positively influence the people with whom he or she comes in contact. Just as a flower exudes its fragrance to whoever comes near or uses it, so love from within radiates towards others and manifests as spontaneous service.

If one considers the evils prevailing in society today, one can easily connect them to the degradation in the value system. A devotee told me about a ninth-grader who had committed suicide because he had not passed his examinations with distinction. Our sense of what is important has become terribly distorted. That is why Amma emphasizes the necessity of bringing up children with spiritual samskāra right from their childhood. It teaches them how to adapt to any circumstance at any time.

There was a married couple who were blessed with a child after many years of fervent prayer. When the child's horoscope was cast, the astrologer warned the parents that the boy would start stealing when he turned 16. When he heard this, the father naturally felt upset. After some time, he hatched a plan. He started buying and bringing home toys, but whenever the boy tried to take any one of them, the father would pretend to become furious. Actually, there was no anger in his heart towards his son, only love, but he wore the mask of anger in order to ensure that his son would never resort to stealing. The father repeated this experiment every day.

When the boy turned 16, the father became anxious. That night, overwhelmed by a sudden and inexplicable urge to steal, the boy went to a jewelry store, intending to purloin some ornaments. But as soon as he stretched out his hand, he remembered his father's angry face and retracted the hand. Thus, the father's disciplining helped to wean the son off a bad habit.

Many ask, "What is the relevance of spirituality in life?" The Sānskṛt word for spirituality is *'adhyātmā,'* which means 'pertaining to the *ātmā* or soul.' The Ātmā is one's own Self; it is the 'I.' So, what people are really asking is, "What is the relevance of one's own Self?" Or, "What is the relevance of the 'I?'"

Actually, the 'I' alone is relevant; everything else is irrelevant. The Vēdāntins recognize the existence of two entities: *'aham'* ('I') and *'idam'* ('this,' i.e. the universe). The former is the support, and the latter, the supported; the seer and the seen. Spirituality is a total separation between the seer and the seen. The seer (individual) realizes that he is not the seen (the objects of the world). This spiritual divorce is a happy, positive and healthy one, wherein there is no enmity between the two entities even after separation. A person like Amma, to whom the Self has been revealed, knows that the world is surreal or unreal, and at the same time, is in love with every object in the world. She is everything; one with the universe. Amma is love itself. To become true love is the essence of spiritual life.

Albert Einstein once said, "A human being is part of the whole, called by us 'universe,' a part limited in time and space. He experiences himself, his thoughts and feelings, as something separate from the rest – a kind of optical delusion of consciousness. This delusion is a kind of prison for us, restricting us to our personal desires and to affection for a few persons nearest to us. Our task must be to free ourselves from this prison by widening our circle of compassion to embrace all living creatures and the whole of nature in its beauty." Yet another Nobel-prize winning scientist, Edwin Schrödinger, remarked, "Consciousness is never experienced in the plural, only in the singular."

Great mystics like Amma have assured us on the strength of their own experiences that we can see all life as an indivisible whole if we cast away the fragmenting instrument of observation, i.e. the ego. Our hearts should not be closed to Amma. It should become a shrine sanctified by Her splendid presence. The more She fills our heart, the less space there will be for the ego.

Visiting Amma's āśram is a celebration. She gives so much love that devotees feel on top of the world. As

Amma's children, should we not also be able to share some of this joy with others? How much satisfaction and happiness there is in sharing!

Once, an elderly man boarded a crowded bus and looked for an empty seat, but could not find one. Seeing the old man, a youngster offered his seat. Both experienced joy. However, the joy of the youth who offered the seat to the elderly man far outweighed the joy of the elder. The joy of sharing is greater than the 'joy' of selfishness any day.

As Amma repeatedly points out, the joy arising from doing a good deed is not experienced in heaven or elsewhere, but here and now. Devotion to Amma essentially includes giving joy to others. It is manifested through loving and serving.

Our body gains value from the service we render others. In other words, what elevates our life is how much we give, not how much we take. Amma reminds us, "While doing sēva, never develop the ego. Don't think that you are going to improve the world. Whatever service we do is for ourselves, for our own expansion." She also points out that for every action, there is a *dṛṣṭa* and an *adṛṣṭa phalam*, literally a 'visible fruit' and an 'invisible fruit.' To cite once again the example of the youth who gave up his seat for the elderly man, the 'visible fruit' is the joy the youth felt when he gave up the seat, and the 'invisible fruit' is the *puṇya* (spiritual merit) he gains as the result of his good karma. Every action we do reaps a dṛṣṭa and an adṛṣṭa phalam.

The *Periya Purāṇam*, the Tamil classic on the Śaiva saints from South India, relates an incident from the life of the saint Sundaramūrti Swāmikaḷ (7th – 8th century CE). The sage was renowned for his mystical powers. Once, when the area around the famed Cidambaram temple was facing a drought, the local prince requested Sundarar to do something about it. The saint immediately prayed, saying that if Lord Śiva showered rains, 12 acres of land would be donated to the temple. As soon as he had finished praying, there was a heavy downpour. But it did not stop pouring even after many days. The prince again called upon Sundarar and beseeched him to pray for the cessation of the rain. Sundarar once again prayed to his beloved Śiva, saying that His temple would gain another 12 acres of land if He stopped the rains. The rains stopped, and thus the temple gained 24 acres of land!

In spite of his intimacy with Lord Śiva, Sundarar was humility personified. One day, as he walked into the Tiruvārūr temple, he saw a group of devotees assembled there. Looking at them, he wondered when he would become a slave to them. Such is the quality of divine love, which finds fulfillment in serving others. This great devotee of Lord Śiva exemplified the truth that love for God is no different from love for His creation.

In the early days, whenever we went out for programs, Amma and Her children would take public transportation. It was only after a few years that the āśram received its first vehicle, which a devotee donated. Some years later, another devotee donated a 'Swaraj Mazda' van. In the back, the first seat on the left, next to the door, was reserved for Amma. A silk cloth was draped over the seat, and everyone else would huddle in whatever little space was available in the van. In those days, I was the only person in the āśram who played the *tabla* and the *mṛdangam*, which Amma humorously referred to as "Vēṇu's children." I looked after them well, carrying them everywhere I went, and even 'dressed' them in special clothes.

Once, after a certain program, everyone boarded the van and waited for Amma to come. I was the last person to board. As soon as I boarded, I noticed the empty chair, reserved for Amma, of course. In that moment, a thought struck me: these instruments, which produce sacred sounds, are worthy of reverence and respect. I could not see them as different from Amma. Without further ado, I placed my carefully-wrapped mṛdangam on Amma's seat. There was an uproar! All the āśram residents seated in the van protested at this seeming blasphemy, this disregard for Amma's seat; some even threatened to throw the mṛdangam out. I stood my ground, refusing to move the mṛdangam away.

At this point, Amma reached the van. "Children, what is the problem?" Someone explained to Amma what I had done. At once, Amma said, "So what? The mṛdangam is Amma; it is Goddess Saraswatī Herself. We should treat it with utmost reverence. Vēṇu-*mōn* (son) has done nothing wrong."

Feeling vindicated, I removed the mṛdangam and let Amma sit there on the seat. She had proven, yet again, that She understood Her son's mind. Not only that, Amma had proclaimed the sublime truth that divinity is immanent in everything.

It would not be an exaggeration to say that Amma has been the greatest advocate of my music. She would often praise my singing. Almost always, whenever famous musicians visited the āśram to perform for Amma, She would say, "Call Vēṇu-mōn. Ask him to come and sing." Amma sees everyone as Her child. She is *'carācara jananī,'* mother of all moving and unmoving beings. Nevertheless, She evinces a soft spot for Her āśram children, praising them and their talents to visiting devotees. Although She is a stern Guru, who never hesitates to cut us down to size whenever we become egoistic, She has another side, too:

that of a mother who is proud of Her children. By Her grace, Her praises or compliments never puffed up my ego.

On occasion, She has acted swiftly to ensure that the hood of my ego does not rise. In the early days, I used to play the *tabla* for Amma. Sometimes, I would get carried away and play a complex rhythmic pattern for a simple bhajan. Right after the bhajan, Amma would turn to me and say in a grave tone, "We haven't come here to become great singers or instrumentalists. Bhajans are a form of sādhana. It should lead us closer to God." Similarly, whenever She sensed that my singing was coming more from the intellect than from the heart, She would say, "Vēṇu, sing from the heart! Sing only for God! This is not a classical performance." This remark would invariably make me feel embarrassed.

And yet, I have never felt that Amma negates classical music or musical passages that demand a high level of technical virtuosity. As with every other deed, She looks at the intent behind the act. She has often asked me to sing '*Sāmagāna Priyē*,' one of my compositions in the Vasanta *rāga*, and other songs that are in the genre of Indian classical music, and which therefore demand knowledge of the nuances of rāgas and a level of technical execution typical of other classical compositions. On some occasions, after I finished singing, Amma has applauded, even while giving darśan. I feel that it might have been because I was so absorbed in the singing that I became oblivious to my surroundings.

In any case, music can raise both the musician and the audience to sublime heights. Even a musician who intends to flaunt his skill and style will find his ego dissolving in the moments the music touches the heart of the rāga; such is the power and glory of music.

'*Samatvam yōga ucyatē*' – 'Even-mindedness is yōga' (*Bhagavad Gītā*, 2.48). Amma echoes this dictum when She says, "We should also be able to see everything as part of the divine principle. Then only can fullness reign. We should be able to see goodness in everything. The honeybees see only the nectar in the flowers and drink it. They do not complain about the thorns in the rose bush. Like the bees, those who see the brighter side of everything get the opportunity to work for the realization of the Self. The attitude of seeing others as one's own Self is, in effect, the state of realization. Just as we do not punish our eyes for failing to see a stump that makes us trip and fall, we should be able to overlook and bear the mistakes of others, seeing them as no different from ourselves. This is the state of realization."

"Lord, grant that I may not so much seek to be loved as to love," prayed Saint Francis of Assisi. Loving is a sādhana for us, whereas for the enlightened, it is a *siddhi*, a fait accompli. As has been noted, Amma sometimes cries when She sees the suffering of others. It is not that Her mind has become emotional, like ours. The mind of the evolved soul is like a mirror. The reflection of a devotee's pain does not affect the mirror, just as a flying bird does not leave a trail in the sky. Similarly, Amma is not affected by the sadness and pain of others; She only reflects it. She is, in fact, bliss personified. Ācārya Śankara's lines in *Bhaja Gōvindam* come to mind.

> *yasya brahmaṇi ramatē cittam*
> *nandati nandati nandatyēva*
> Only he whose mind steadily delights in Brahman
> enjoys bliss alone. (20)

When Rāmānuja, saint and foremost exponent of *Viśiṣṭādvaita* (the philosophy of qualified non-dualism), was about to be initiated into a sacred mantra, his Guru warned him not to reveal it to anyone else; if he did, Rāmānuja would be condemned to eternal damnation whereas the recipient of the mantra would enjoy heavenly bliss. As soon as he had been initiated into the mantra, Rāmānuja rushed into the temple courtyard and, calling all and sundry, disclosed the sacred mantra, '*Ōm namō nārāyaṇāya*,' to them. His Guru pretended to be enraged, and asked Rāmānuja to account for his disobedience. Rāmānuja's reply was that if he could ensure the spiritual salvation of others by his own damnation, he was ready to do so.

Such is the flaming love saints have for humanity. It can never be extinguished. In the *Vivēkacūḍāmaṇi*, Śankarācārya describes the Guru as *'ahaituka dayā sindhu'* – 'one whose infinite mercy knows no reason' (33).

During Her early days, Amma would wander in ecstasy, hugging trees and plants, and embracing sand and seawater. She sees all beings, including animals and insects, as extensions of Her pure Self. Amma shows us that there is no limit to our capacity to love. We must rise to the level of loving universally; i.e. becoming one with love itself. Through Her own experience, Amma has realized that the real nature of the world is Brahman – *'prapañcasvarūpam brahma.'*

The renowned Russian writer Fyodor Dostoyevsky memorably said, "Love all that has been created by God, both the whole and every grain of sand. Love every leaf and every ray of light. Love the beasts and the birds, love the plants, love every separate fragment, you will understand the mystery of the whole resting in God."

When we observe nature, we can see the remarkable trait of effortless expansion. Grass does not try to grow; it just grows. Flowers just bloom and birds just fly. The sun shines naturally and the stars sparkle effortlessly. Nature's intelligence functions spontaneously and effortlessly because all of nature is held together by the energy of love.

Amma says, "Children, you only know love in the external world, which is between two humans, but for Amma, there is no limit to the love flowing from her towards all beings in this universe. In the external world, people love each other for their own selfish interests. Amma's love doesn't expect anything in return. If you want to love, do so openly. If there is love, it must be open and pure."

Swāmi Rāma Tīrtha narrates a story on the necessity of wishing others well. Once, an ascetic gave a merchant a magic item that could fulfill any desire. There was a catch: his neighbor would get double of whatever the devotee desired. The man soon gained money, elephants, horses, cattle... and his neighbor gained twice as much of all this wealth. This was too much for the merchant to bear. After some deliberation, he came up with a plan. He asked to lose one eye. His wish was granted, and his neighbor lost both his eyes. He then wished for one of his arms and one of his legs to be broken. The result was that both the legs and arms of his neighbor broke. In spite of his own dysfunction, the man gloated in the misery of his neighbor. Soon after this, the man became ill and his body was paralyzed. He was no longer able to use the one hand

and leg that had been functional, and he also lost vision in the only eye that could see. He tried to use the magic article to heal himself, but was told that this was not possible, as it would mean that his neighbor would gain four eyes, hands and legs. Stalemated, the man had no choice but to ask for one good eye, one good hand and one good leg. Simultaneously, his neighbor recovered completely! For the rest of his life, the merchant had to contend with his deformities.

Philosophically speaking, human beings can be classified into four categories: 1. those in whom only the brains are developed; 2. those in whom the heart alone is developed; 3. those in whom neither the brain nor the heart is developed; and 4. those in whom both the heart and the brain are equally and perfectly developed. People like Rāma, Kṛṣṇa, Amma, Ramaṇa Maharṣi and Jesus Christ belong to the last category.

About 30 years ago, a touching incident took place in Amṛtapuri. It is the story of how a family became ardent devotees of Amma. The parents had two sons, who loved each other greatly. If the younger brother was ill, the elder brother would take care of him by bathing and feeding him. One day, the younger brother suddenly died, owing to brain hemorrhage. This shocked the whole family, especially the elder brother, who became mentally unbalanced after this incident. He started acting strangely, and his parents were immersed in gloom. One night, the mother dreamed that a woman in white was standing in front of her, and standing next to this woman was her dead son! The woman beckoned her elder son to come near, and when he went over, she told him to look at her face and smile. He looked at her face and smiled. With this, the dream ended. The mother woke up smiling. Later, she related this dream to her husband, but both of them dismissed it as a dream of no significance. However, this dream kept recurring during the next four days, leading them to conclude that the dream was significant.

Soon after these dreams, when the family was returning home on a bus one day, a woman came up to them and started talking to them about Amma and the Vaḷḷikkāvu āśram. When they heard this, they felt an inexplicable and strong urge to meet Amma and see Her āśram. They went to Amṛtapuri the very next day. When they arrived at the āśram, Amma was giving darśan to devotees. As soon as they reached the entrance of the darśan hut, Amma called them and asked the elder son to look at Her face and smile, just as She had done in the mother's dream. The boy did as Amma instructed, and he was completely cured. The family became ardent devotees of Amma.

How can one explain this? Such is the *śakti*, or power, of a mahātmā. It can do anything. We can also attain this state if we dedicate ourselves to God-realization instead of wasting our energy in trivial pursuits.

When Jesus Christ once invited a man to follow Him, the man demurred, saying that he first wanted to bury his father, who had just died. Christ then told him, "Let the dead bury their own dead, but you go and proclaim the kingdom of God." By 'dead,' Christ was referring to people who are not alive to the Spirit, i.e. those who are not pursuing any spiritual discipline. By asking the man to proclaim the kingdom of God, Christ was asking him to take to the spiritual path and discover God. The man heeded His words and became a disciple of Christ.

Meditation and selfless actions are complementary. Performing selfless actions deepens one's meditation. The deeper meditation becomes, the more one can tap into reserves of energy to love and help others. Śrī Rāmakṛṣṇa used to sing these lines from a popular Bengali hymn:

> Dive deep, O mind, dive deep
> Into the ocean of God's beauty;
> If you descend to the uttermost depths,
> There you will find the gem of love.

7
"Do they all worship you?"

Picture the guileless smile of a baby. That smile is an expression of happiness and contentment. The naturalness and spontaneity of the smile make no demands, and yet, the smile touches the heart of the onlooker, such is its purity. Truly, there is nothing so disarming as innocence.

Amma's spontaneity unfailingly charms and wins over even the driest cynics. Once, after She had landed in India from an overseas tour and was emerging from the airport, She saw a swarm of people – mostly devotees but also some reporters. Spontaneously, Amma brought Her palms together prayerfully and smiled lovingly at the masses. One curious reporter pointedly asked Her, alluding to the people who were gazing at Her with undisguised reverence, "Do they all worship you?"

Without missing a beat, Amma responded, with Her hands still in prayerful pose, "No, I worship them."

This was not just brilliant repartee. It was a simple expression of Amma's philosophy expressed in a nutshell. As has been mentioned before, it is because She sees everyone as Her Self, as God, that She loves and worships them. Her sensitivity to everything, living and inert, comes naturally to Her, and that is what makes Amma one of the greatest spiritual masters of all time.

Amma is a source of marvel for many, both in the East and the West. News reports of Her programs often reflect a sense of wonder at the phenomenal stamina that enables Her to give darśan to thousands daily. *Münchner Merkur*, a German newspaper, ran an article on Amma. A translated excerpt of the article is reproduced below:

> *Tirelessly, the tiny woman dressed in white holds one person after another to Her chest, whispering something comforting into each one's ears. She is always smiling... She embraces up to 15,000 people a day, every day. Hardly anybody is capable of putting into words what is happening to him or her when being hugged by Amma.*

Amma's indefatigability is an expression not just of Her unconditional love but also of Her total dedication and surrender to Her mission of loving and serving others. She maintains the same format in all Her programs: bhajans, meditation, *mānasa pūja* (prayer through visualization) and darśan. In Her satsangs, She also incorporates a prayer that the congregation repeats after Her:

> *śakti tā jagadambē, prēmam tā jagadambē,*
> *viśvāsam tannenne rakṣikku jagadambē*
> O Mother of the Universe, give me strength and love.
> Give me faith, and thus protect me.

It is a prayer for devotion and surrender. One of the most celebrated verses from the *Bhagavad Gītā* exhorts the devotee to surrender to God unreservedly:

> *sarvadharmān parityajya māmēkam śaraṇam vraja*
> *aham tvā sarva pāpēbhyō mōkṣayiṣyāmi mā śucaḥ*
> Relinquishing all dharmas, take refuge in Me alone.
> I will liberate you from all sins. Grieve not. (18.66)

This is Lord Kṛṣṇa's guarantee to Arjuna, who is representative of all jīvas. Thus, the Lord's assurance holds true for each one of us. By 'relinquishing all dharmas,' Kṛṣṇa does not mean that we should give up all action or that we should forsake dharma. Dharma is the law of being, which makes an object what it is. For example, heat is the dharma of fire, and sweetness, the dharma of sugar. If fire were cold or sugar were sour, it would not be fire or sugar. The dharma of humanity is divine consciousness; in other words, the Truth.

Is this what the Lord is asking us to forsake? It cannot be. The fact that He has used the plural form of the word ('dharmas') is telling. All of us are identified with the body, mind and intellect, and therefore, our sense of who we are is tied down strongly to these limited identifications. This composite sense of individuality is nothing but the ego. What Śrī Kṛṣṇa wants us to abandon are these subsidiary identifications with the body, mind and intellect. When one does that, one effectively abandons the sense of 'doer-ship' or agency.

The point here is that the performance of one's duties is not the be-all and end-all of spiritual striving; it is dedicating all action to God ('take refuge in Me alone') so that one may gain *īśvara-kṛpā*, or divine grace. Amma often reiterates this point in Her talks – the need to work in all earnestness and to strive for grace all the time. This prayerful attitude helps one to do any kind of work while maintaining one's focus on the ultimate dharma of liberation.

The phantom of doer-ship possesses all but the rare being. Śrī Ramaṇa Maharṣi explains through the analogy of a *gōpuram*, the temple tower, how ludicrous the idea is. At the base of some gōpurams, there is a sculpted figure that looks as if it is bearing the weight of the entire tower on its shoulders. The truth, of course, is that the tower is resting on its foundations, which go deep into the earth. Similarly, the person who thinks that he does this or that harbors a grandiose delusion. The spiritual seeker works towards releasing this false perception and resting on the foundation of Truth.

Swāmi Rāma Tīrtha relates a story about the 'imp of doer-ship:'

Once, there was a man so clever as to reproduce himself to such perfection that you could not tell the reproduction from the original. He knew that the angel of death was coming for him and as he did not know just what to do to avoid the angel, he finally settled upon what might be termed an able device. He reproduced himself a dozen times. Now when the angel of death came, he could not tell which was the real person and, therefore, did not take any. The angel returned to God and asked Him what to do, and after a consultation returned to the earth to try again to take this man and remarked, "Dear, you are wonderfully clever; why, that is just the way you have made these figures, but there is one thing wherein you have erred, there is just one fault."

The original man immediately jumped up and asked suddenly, "In what, in what have I erred?"

And the angel said, "By asking in what way you were wrong," singling out the clever man from the mute statues. "By doing so, you revealed your egoistic sense of doer-ship." Death then took away the original man.

Striving for divine grace makes one more self-effacing. It keeps the mind away from negativity and thoughts of sin, and the very effort to become eligible for grace gradually removes the effects of past transgressions. Likewise, practicing surrender inculcates the spirit of love, devotion and faith.

Amma inspires people to act with an attitude of surrender. She has simplified meditation techniques, taught easy-to-follow pūjas to thousands, guided them in simple yet soulful prayers, and imparted spiritual energy to millions by Her mere touch.

Amma has also introduced a simple yet powerful '*Mā-Ōm*' meditation technique. Mentally synchronizing the sound '*Mā*' while inhaling and '*Ōm*' while exhaling has a powerful and profound effect, especially when practiced regularly. 'Mā' represents divine love, and 'Ōm' represents divine light. Amma says that this method of breathing can be practiced anywhere and by anyone.

Similarly, to the devout, Amma teaches easy ways to perform a pūja. At the outset, She instructs them to visualize their '*iṣṭa dēvatā*' (preferred form of divinity) seated on a royal throne. Using their powers of visualization and imagination, devotees perform *pādābhiṣēkam* (ceremonial washing of the deity's feet) and then proceed to dress and adorn the deity. Thereafter, they feed the deity and offer the ārati flame to it, all the while chanting their mantra or speaking to the iṣṭa dēvatā. Here is pūja at its most intimate and vivid. Can there be a better way of bringing people closer to God?

Amma's darśan not only imparts joy and energy, it also demonstrates sēva at its purest: relentlessly giving without expectation of return; in other words, perfect surrender. Lord Kṛṣṇa's statement on selfless service is reassuring:

> *nēhābhikramanāśōSsti pratyavāyō na vidyatē*
> *svalpamapyasya dharmasya trāyatē mahatō bhayāt*
> In this (spiritual path of karma yōga), there is
> no waste of the unfinished attempt, nor is there
> production of contrary results. Even very little
> of this dharma protects one from the great fear.
> (*Bhagavad* Gītā, 2.40)

In karma yōga, every effort results in purification of the heart; it is not like a house left unroofed; because it cannot be lived in, it is a 'waste of the unfinished attempt.' Also, selfless service does not produce 'contrary results,' which will be the certain outcome of taking the wrong medicine, for example. In this way, Lord Kṛṣṇa distinguishes karma yōga from other spheres of action. Finally, He guarantees that a follower of the path of karma yōga will be protected from the 'great fear' of being caught in the wheel of samsāra.

Despite the overwhelming demands on Her time, Amma still meets and interacts with each and every person who lines up for darśan. On average, each person might get only a few seconds with Amma, and yet in this span of time, Amma is able to communicate soulfully with each one. She receives hundreds of letters from devotees daily, and She finds time to read all of them.

There have been innumerable instances when devotees from various parts of the world have experienced their prayers being answered. This is possible because She is pure energy, which transcends time and space, and simultaneously accesses each and every one who yearns for Her grace.

A devotee in his early 60s who had rheumatoid arthritis was staying in a seaside city. Winter conditions and humidity aggravated his problem one night. He was alone in his apartment; his family had gone on a short vacation. The pain started early in the evening, and by the time he went to bed, the agony became unbearable. He tried to get some sleep and kept turning from one side to the other, but the pain worsened, making it impossible to sleep. Finally, at about midnight, unable to endure the suffering, he cried out, "Amma, what is this? Why me?" Strangely, after he had called out to Amma, he fell asleep. He then dreamed of Her. Standing beside him, She told him, "Son, you had better sleep on your back." The devotee woke up and checked the time; he had not slept for more than 10 minutes. He got up and reflected on the dream. Because it was Amma who had advised him, he lay on his back, a position he had never liked.

When he woke up, it was 6 a.m. The alarm clock had gone off at the pre-set time of 5 a.m. He recalled the events of the night – the pain, his calling out to Amma, the dream in which She advised him, and the sound sleep that followed. He felt overwhelmed by Amma's compassion in relieving his pain. He was also able to go to work on time. What he did not realize then was that Amma had administered a therapy that completely healed him. In due course, he realized that the chronic problem, which had been haunting him for a decade, had vanished totally! More than a decade has passed since the healing, and the pain has not returned.

Amma also expresses compassion on a more practical and manifest level. In the past, people used to line up for darśan tokens. Now, after Amma's intervention, devotees remain seated on chairs, and volunteers give them tokens on a first-come-first-served basis.

Many devotees also used to lose their footwear, which they would leave outside the hall where Amma's program was being conducted. Now, people can wear their shoes or sandals inside the hall. For Amma, orthodoxy is subservient to Her children's comfort and convenience.

Yet another recent innovation was the projection of the bhajan lyrics and their translation on large screens. So, not only can devotees sing along, they can also appreciate the beautiful teachings that the bhajans convey.

Amma also knows that most people are choosy about food. Now, in both Amṛtapuri and Her program venues elsewhere, devotees can choose from different cuisines. This is not to indulge their petty whims, but to help minimize distractions and make them comfortable.

With all these changes and innovations in place, there's little room for complaint! With so many concessions in place, we are now free to concentrate on imbibing the milk of Amma's love and compassion.

Amma has also introduced more radical changes. One of the most notable is popularizing the chanting of the *Laḷitā Sahasranāma*, the thousand names of the Divine Mother. In bygone times, this sacred litany used to be chanted only by Brāhmins, mainly priests. Naturally, when Amma encouraged Her children to chant it daily, some people reacted against this perceived affront to orthodoxy.

A self-appointed guardian of tradition once went to meet Amma and asked Her, "Amma, the *Laḷitā Sahasranāma* was traditionally only chanted by a select group. You have made it accessible to the masses. Shouldn't we respect and safeguard tradition?"

Amma's reply was telling. "Son, God Himself told me to offer it to everyone for the good of the world!"

Hopefully, the gentleman understood the point behind Amma's seeming audacity – that the right to determine what is right is the prerogative of a Guru, or a person who is one with God. In any case, given that the *Laḷitā Sahasranāma* is a tribute to Her, the Divine Mother, She ought to have every right to decide what to do with it, shouldn't She?

Furthermore, this episode begs the question: who really is the Divine Mother? She is divine consciousness, which is our very nature. Amma wants us to realize our divine nature, and has directed us to chant the *Laḷitā Sahasranāma* daily. By invoking the divine names of the Goddess, we are connecting with our own divine nature.

A devotee had an experience during one of Amma's Madurai programs. A devotee of Lord Śiva, he had been brought up from a young age to worship Lord Śiva and Goddess Mīnākṣī, commonly known as Madurai Mīnākṣī. He had also worshipped at the Madurai Mīnākṣī temple many times. Just before attending Amma's program in the morning, he had gone to that temple.

It was a special day for pūjas, and the emerald idol of the Goddess was shining with great parrot-green resplendence. Reveling in this mesmerizing sight, he then drove to Amma's program. For this devotee, Amma and Madurai Mīnākṣī, his iṣṭa dēvatā, are one, and he used to worship Amma as such.

When he entered the tent, he saw that Amma had just walked onto the stage. She looked at the crowd of devotees and greeted them by holding Her hands aloft prayerfully. As this devotee looked at Amma, he was awe-struck by what he saw. Amma's face and hands were green – the same shade of green that he had seen on Madurai Mīnākṣī. For a moment, he thought he was dreaming and was about to dismiss the sight as a figment of his imagination. He turned his gaze away. When he looked again, it was not just the color of Her skin, Her face and hands bore an uncanny resemblance to Madurai Mīnākṣī. It was as if Amma was confirming this devotee's faith that She was indeed one with his iṣṭa dēvatā.

Sometimes, during Amma's programs, there is a mass chanting of the *Laḷitā Aṣṭōttaram* and the *Laḷitā Triśatī*, apart from the *Laḷitā Sahasranāma* arcana. Although there are different *dhyāna śḷōkas* (invocatory verses) for the *Triśatī* and the *Sahasranāma*, the dhyāna śḷōka of the *Laḷitā Sahasranāma* ('*Sindūrāruṇavigrahām...*') is chanted before both the *Triśatī* and the *Sahasranāma* during Amma's programs. During darśan, when someone pedantically asked Amma why the same dhyāna śḷōka was being chanted before both the *Laḷitā Sahasranāma* and the *Triśatī* when there were different dhyāna śḷōkas for both, She replied, "What matters is the devotion with which the sacred names are chanted, not which dhyāna śḷōka is chanted. In any case, whether it is the *Sahasranāma* or the *Triśatī*, it is Dēvī who is being worshipped. I decided that it was enough to chant the same dhyāna śḷōka for both!"

On another occasion, Amma again demonstrated Her classy chutzpah when a Brāhmin scholar questioned Amma: "What is the Brahmasthānam temple's *mūla mantra* (root mantra)?"

Her rejoinder was swift: "That mantra needs to be disclosed only to the priest of the Brahmasthānam temple, right?"

As far as Amma is concerned, the Truth is not the exclusive preserve of a few. Just as every Master has interpreted age-old teachings to suit the age they lived in, Amma has, through Her initiatives, defined the practices best suited to our times.

For example, She has undermined the chauvinistic underpinnings of religious dogma by upholding the equality of men and women. She maintains that man and woman are like the two wings of a bird. No side can claim to be superior to the other; rather, they are complementary.

To the question, "Is God a man or a woman?" Amma says, "The answer to that question is that God is neither male nor female because divinity is none of the sensual objects we perceive. In another sense, God is both male and female because the divine is everything." As one wit put it, God is neither a mister nor a miss but a mystery!

With unimpeachable logic, Amma brushed away the cobwebs of repressive ideology, and advocated a more egalitarian approach to the treatment of the sexes. Her efforts to give women an equal status in society have been like a whiff of fresh air in today's world. She has initiated several measures in Her own organizations to give women their rightful position. For example, Amma has inducted brahmacāriṇīs as priests in Brahmasthānam temples. When asked if She approved of woman devotees of all ages going to Śabarimala, the hill-top temple in Kēraḷa dedicated to Lord Ayyappa, Amma said that there should be no restriction for women of any age to pray there or at any other shrine. When further questioned on how the status quo could be changed, Amma replied, "It is for the *ācāryas* (religious preceptors) to effect the change."

To call a spade a spade, and yet refrain from enforcing Her views on others — this remarkable blend of candor and humility is characteristic of Amma's style. She takes us to Truth, helping us to transcend all distractions and man-made interpretations of religion. However, She does so with utmost respect and love for all.

8
"Want to make the Lord break His vow?"

Some people have misconceptions about *bhakti* (devotion) and *bhaktas* (devotees). They associate bhakti with places of worship, such as temples, or associated paraphernalia like the conch or the bells sounded during religious rituals. Similarly, they think of a bhakta as someone who rises early in the morning, bathes, visits and worships at the temple, receives prasād from the priest, daubs his forehead with sandal paste/*kumkum* (saffron powder)/sacred ash, and places above the ear or on the head flowers given by the priest.

The Sānskṛt word '*bhakti*' is derived from the root '*bhaj*,' which means to adore or to worship (serve) with love. To put it briefly, anything done with selfless love – whether it is worship, meditation, prayer, pūja or service – is an aspect of bhakti.

Essentially, bhakti is the feeling of being one with God and acting accordingly. A bhakta constantly lives with the awareness that God knows and is aware of all his/her actions, be they thoughts, words or deeds.

In the *Nārada Bhakti Sūtras*, after presenting the characteristics of bhakti that various other preceptors have given, Śrī Nārada presents his own:

nāradastu tadarpitākhilācāratā
tadvismaraṇē paramavyākulatēti

> Indeed, Nārada is of the opinion that the characteristics of devotion are dedication of all activities to God and extreme anguish if He is forgotten (19).

For those who think bhakti is all about rapturous bliss, Nārada's explanation might seem like a radical re-evaluation. In this sage's experience, bhakti evokes extremes of emotions – supreme bliss when in touch with the divine, and total anguish when the connection is lost. Such has been the experience of other devotees par excellence, too. While reminiscing about Her sādhana phase, Amma said that if She could not remember God, the pain and agony She experienced in the heart would be unbearable. If She did not chant His name while walking, She would retrace Her steps and chant the names. Only then would She move ahead. Similarly, during His period of austerities, Śrī Rāmakṛṣṇa Paramahamsa used to feel intense angst when His mind left Dēvī for even a moment. He likened the torment to having his heart wrung, as if it were wet cloth.

Most of us are unlikely to have encountered such extremes of devotion. To help us understand it, Amma says, "Children, if you take a fish out from water and put it on the shore, it will desperately gasp and struggle until it is thrown back into the water. Similar is the restlessness and pain in the heart of the bhakta."

Spiritual masters like Śrī Śankara have described true devotion as unbroken or indivisible. It is 'like an unbroken stream of oil' – '*tailadhārāvat.*' The love in a devotee's heart is an unbroken stream flowing continuously towards the Lord, culminating in God-realization.

The *Purāṇas* and *Itihāsas* depict a devotee thus: copious tears flow down his cheeks as he worships his beloved deity. Overcome by emotions, he is unable to speak. He is unaffected by anything else. Even if all the fortunes of the world tried to lure him, he would not even glance in their direction, for he has discovered joy within himself.

The words of mahātmās and sacred texts like the *Nārada Bhakti Sūtras* and the *Bhāgavata Purāṇa* provide authoritative expositions on bhakti. The *śāstras* (scriptures) give equal importance to all types of sādhana, duly considering the merits of each. As Amma says, "One person may like *dōśa* (Indian pancake) whereas another may prefer banana and *pūṭṭu* (South Indian breakfast item made from rice flour). You cannot say that one is better than the other or that one thing is good, and the other, bad. Different people have different tastes."

The heart of a bhakta is saturated with God. He surrenders and offers his individuality entirely to the Lord.

This does not mean that he disappears, but that he lives in a sublime state of inner union with God. In that state, there is no duality – the distinctions of Bhagavān and bhakta, Lord and devotee, are completely effaced. *Dvaita* (duality) culminates in *advaita* (non-duality). This abidance in non-duality is the pinnacle of the *bhakti mārga*, the path of devotion.

Even though Amma is one with God, She still prays soulfully to the divine when She sings bhajans. She calls and cries out to Dēvī or Kṛṣṇa. This ecstatic outpouring of love is an awe-inspiring demonstration of devotion, which inspires us to open our hearts in yearning for God.

Sugar, by itself, can never enjoy or experience its sweetness, but ants can. The *bhāva* (mood or attitude) of bhakti is so unique that only a true bhakta can enjoy its sweetness. Bhakti is nothing but an expression of the pure bhāva of love towards the divine. Also, without *bhāvanā* (imagination), there is no bhakti. So fervid was the devotion of the *gōpīs* (milkmaids) that they saw Kṛṣṇa's yellow robes in the *kadamba* flowers and His footfalls in every indentation on the ground; they heard His melodious flute in the susurration of the leaves; and they felt His presence in every nook and corner of Vṛndāvan. They even sanctified commerce by labeling the wares they sold with one of the Lord's many names. Today, the gōpīs' all-embracing adoration has become a byword for true love.

Amma also exhorts us to pray with devotion. "Chanting the Lord's name without any feeling is dry and mechanical. One should chant with the bhāva of love. Children, always pray, imagining your iṣṭa dēvatā against the backdrop of nature."

Amma points out to Her children that bhakti is the easiest way to God-realization. Though the *Bhāgavata Purāṇa* describes many types of sādhana, it gives more importance to emotions (feelings) and desires, which are capitalized upon in the path of devotion. This path is the most accessible and practical because anyone, irrespective of race, age or gender, can follow it easily. In the *Vivēkacūḍāmaṇi*, Śrī Śankarācārya declares:

> *mokṣakāraṇasāmagryām bhaktirēva garīyasī*
> *svasvarūpānusandhānam bhaktirityabhidhīyatē*
> Among things conducive to Liberation, devotion alone holds the supreme place. The seeking after one's real nature is designated as devotion. (31)

Other paths are fraught with peril. In the path of karma, one should act without the sense of doer-ship or expectation of result, which is extremely difficult for an ordinary person. One who follows the *jñāna mārga*, the path of knowledge, finds the going even tougher. At every turn, he has to practice negation ("this is not It") in order to distinguish between the eternal and the ephemeral. In a bid for transcendence, he has to constantly remind himself, "I am not the mind or the body. I am not the intelligence." He has to practice *śama* and *dama*, mind-control and sense-control. He has to live in an isolated place and follow many other restrictions. He has to perform intense penance in the presence of his Guru.

In contrast, the path of bhakti is not hemmed in by so many do-s and don'ts. One can repeat (remember) the Lord's name anywhere.

There is another reason why bhakti is considered the easiest path. Of all the human feelings and emotions, love is the safest and noblest, and bhakti is based on love. Everyone, without exception, has feelings. Anyone who claims to have no feelings or emotions is not speaking the truth. Even the most stone-hearted person will have tender feelings for his or her loved ones.

When we are young, we run to our mother with our problems and complaints. After we grow up and get married, we turn to our spouse. A chaste wife longs to see her husband who has not yet returned home. Love can change and transform the most hardened criminal or the cruelest person. There is love among other beings, too. A newly-hatched bird is anxious to see its mother. A weary and hungry calf yearns for its mother cow. Even non-living objects like iron, when magnetized, attract each other. Gravitational force is another instance of this truth. Bhakti is nothing but the spiritual principle of such attraction. It is the force behind the evolution of the jivātmā to the Paramātmā.

The āśram, i.e. Amma's presence, is a conducive arena for nurturing devotion and other qualities that accelerate spiritual progress. In the early days, life in the āśram teemed with adversity. There was precious little by way of food, shelter or clothing, the necessities of life. Amma's love and compassion were literally our lifeline, nourishing our nascent spiritual longings.

Not only that, in my callowness, I was often intimidated by many people around Amma. Suguṇānandan-acchan, Amma's father, initially did not approve of young men staying or loitering around his house; this was perfectly understandable, considering that he had three unmarried daughters, and the conservative mores of the community Amma's family lived in frowned upon unseemly interaction between the sexes. Damayanti-amma, Amma's mother, was loving but deeply orthodox. For example, if you wanted to help her in the kitchen, you would first have to bathe and then salute the kitchen fire before commencing the cooking.

I had to do all this because I used to help her in the kitchen. Assisting her was an exacting task that demanded a lot of attentiveness. And then there were householder devotees who would order us around, seeing us as no more than menial servants of the āśram.

In addition, each visit to Amma meant a walk from Vaḷḷikkāvu junction to the boat jetty, which invariably involved quietly enduring a lot of verbal abuse and jeers from the villagers on the path. In hindsight, it is obvious that these factors helped us acquire humility and equanimity of mind in all circumstances, without which no aspirant can progress spiritually.

At that time, apart from Amma and the āśram, the only other place where I could take refuge was the house of Saraswati-amma (or "Vallyammacci," as I called her). My mother's elder sister, she had raised me after my mother died in my infancy. Her house has been blessed by Amma's presence many times. In fact, She even used to stay there, sometimes for up to three or four days at a stretch.

In those days, owing to Amma's inspiration, I used to do intense penance. I actually believed that Brahman, or the Supreme, was within easy reach, and would spend hours every day in meditation, trying to still, and, thus, go beyond my mind. Sometimes, I would even forgo Amma's company in order to do more meditation. Such was the intensity of my desire to realize the Goal. A few of my family members were even convinced that I was crazy, perhaps affected by black magic. They would say, "Vēṇu was such a normal fellow. Now look what has happened to him!"

Once, I went to the stream behind Vallyammacci's house to take a bath at 3 a.m. Thereafter, I went straight to the pūja room and started practicing some *yōgāsanas* (yōgic postures). At one point, I was performing the *śīrṣāsana*, the headstand. At about four in the morning, one of my cousins who used to wake up early to pray walked into the pūja room. She almost jumped out of her skin when she saw me standing on my head, with my feet at her eye level. She started wailing loudly, "O Kāḷī! O Dēvī! What has happened to this boy? Has my Vēṇu become deranged? O Kṛṣṇa! O Śiva! Please do something!" I jumped upright and bolted from the room before her lamentations became too hysterical!

In those days, I was convinced that it was within Amma's power to grant me spiritual liberation, and failing to realize the Goal, I would become very angry with Amma! In fact, I used to fight with Her over this. This was not for any material benefits but because I could not understand why She was withholding the fruit of spiritual realization even after much assiduous striving. Often, after these Mother-

and-son spats, She would console me by saying that spiritual striving will yield dividends in due course, but urged me to be patient and reasonable. She pointed out how aspirants through the ages had performed tapas for years, if not lifetimes, for just one glimpse of the Divine, and that I should, therefore, not be unreasonable in my demands. She kept reassuring me that She was with me.

One day, after quarreling with Her over the same issue yet again, I walked off in a huff. This time, Amma did not come after me. She must have felt that my childish willfulness and obstinacy were best dealt with by silence and indifference. We were in Vallyammacci's house then. Sulking, I left the house by the back door and went to sit under a coconut tree by the stream to meditate. I resolved not to get up until I had attained Self-realization or until Amma called me... whichever came first! My attempts at concentration were broken by thoughts of how hungry I was and by worries over why Amma had not called me or come to me yet. I sat there for one-and-a-half hours.

Then, fatigued, I stood up and walked into the house. There were many people there, both my immediate family members as well as some relatives. As soon as I entered, they shot me a puzzled look. Some covered their noses. A few asked, "What is that dreadful stench?" After some time, an uncle noticed the back of my dhōti. He said,

"Look, Vēṇu's backside is smeared with excreta." I peered behind – it was true; I had unknowingly sat on a pile of turd under the coconut tree... and not been aware of it at all! So much for the fragrance of meditation! Amma peered at my derrière and burst into peals of blissful laughter. Seeing Her laugh, my inner conflicts were resolved and I broke out laughing, too!

If I were in the āśram following one of those spats with Amma, I would deliberately stay away from Her for a few days. Whenever I saw Her coming my way, I would steer away! Although this was my childish and immature way of 'getting back' at Her, the separation from Amma would cause unimaginable anguish in my heart. Sometimes, when the torment became unbearable, I would run to the kaḷari and sing my heart out, belting out bhajans like '*Harē Murārē*' and '*Harē Rāma*' at the top of my voice. All the pent-up pain and anguish would express itself through the music, and sometimes, when I found no relief from the intense suffering, I would cry out at the top of my voice, "Ammaaaa!...." Invariably, at this point, when my heart was broken, unable to bear any more anguish, Amma would run to me and, cradling me on Her shoulders, console me with sweet words of motherly love: "My son, Vēṇu, my darling son, my sweet child, don't cry, Amma is with you..."

I would remain sobbing in Her arms for 10 – 15 minutes, until all my anguish had been spent through tears.

Śrī Rāmakṛṣṇa Paramahamsa has said that in the evolving relationship between God and devotee, God first acts like a magnet, drawing the devotee closer. Thereafter, it is the devotee who has to attract God towards himself by his love and longing. Here, two strands of bhakti are apparent – the devotee's love for the Lord is bhakti or devotion; the Lord's affection for His devotee is compassion. Devotion cannot blossom without the nourishment of divine compassion. Thus, bhakti is that noble sentiment that binds the bhakta with Bhagavān.

The biography of Śrī Rāmakṛṣṇa Paramahamsa also records how He used to wait anxiously for the arrival of spiritual aspirants. The same was true of Amma. In the early days, She would wait by the bank of the backwaters, swaying left and right in a trance. By divine intuition, She would know when one of Her spiritual children was going to arrive, and would eagerly wait for him. Similarly, whenever we were leaving, Amma would wipe our faces clean, comb our hair and apply sandal paste on our foreheads, as though we were young children, and then accompany us to the backwaters to see us off. Indeed, we were just like children then. During that period, we were so intoxicated by Amma's divine love that we could never take care of ourselves, and needed Mother to take care of us.

The love that the Lord has for His devotee is much more intense than what the bhakta feels for God. The story of Bhīṣma is telling. Lord Kṛṣṇa had vowed never to use a weapon in the Kurukṣētra War under any circumstance whatsoever, but Bhīṣma had vowed to make the Lord do so. On the ninth day of the war, Bhīṣma's arrows injured the Lord. Even when blood was dripping from His wounds, Kṛṣṇa continued smiling and steering Arjuna's chariot. But when Bhīṣma injured Arjuna, causing profuse bleeding, the Lord could not abide by it. He took His glorious *sudarśana cakra* (spinning disk-like weapon with serrated edges) and ran towards Bhīṣma, intending to kill him. Thus, the Lord broke His pledge for the sake of both His devotees. Kṛṣṇa not only protected Arjuna from further harm, He also helped to fulfill Bhīṣma's vow even though it meant breaking His own. Truly, Bhagavān's compassion is much greater in magnitude than the bhakta's devotion.

After Amma's 61st birthday celebrations, an āśram resident wrote a letter to Amma, complaining about the behavior of another resident. Owing to a lack of accommodation facilities for the sheer numbers who had come to join the Birthday celebrations, the Kāḷī Temple had been designated a sleeping space for women. Some of these women had travelled long distances to see Amma, and had to wait many hours before they received Amma's darśan. By the time they retired to the Kāḷī Temple for the night, it was almost two in the morning. One āśram resident, whose sēva was cleaning the temple, had woken them all up barely an hour after they went to sleep and shooed them out of the temple. Not only that, seeing their slippers strewn haphazardly on the temple steps, she had impatiently hurled them all away in order to clean the steps.

When Amma heard this, Her expression became grave. Looking at the person concerned, She first said, "Don't ever go into the Kāḷī Temple again. You don't need to do sēva there anymore." After a few moments, Amma said, "I don't mind it if someone does something bad or says something bad to me. But if they offend my devotees, I will not tolerate it!" She then spoke of how treating guests as God was a central tenet of Sanātana Dharma, a belief expressed in the saying, "*Atithi dēvō bhava*." Amma said that the resident's action had not only been a transgression of India's traditional cultural ethos, but had betrayed a cruel lack of compassion. She said that serving guests with sincere love would have been a far better pūja to Mother Kāḷī than cleaning the temple. The all-knowing Amma also pointed out that each pair of slippers that the āśram resident had thrown away may have cost only between 100 and 150 rupees, but this sum was a large one for the poor women, who would have to work hard to earn enough money to buy another pair.

In the *Śrīmad Bhāgavatam*, Śrī Kṛṣṇa tells Uddhava,

> *nirapēkṣam munim śāntam*
> *nirvairam samadarśanam*
> *anuvrajāmyaham nityam*
> *pūyēyētyanghrirēṇubhiḥ*
>
> I always follow the pure ascetic, who is serene and composed, who expects nothing from anyone, who has enmity towards none, and who sees everyone equally, so that I may be purified by the dust from his feet. (11.14.16)

Amma narrates the story of how Lord Kṛṣṇa once feigned a migraine to show Sage Nārada how elevated the devotion of the gōpīs was. All those around Him were wondering what they could do to alleviate the Lord's pain. When they asked Him, Kṛṣṇa said, "Only if the dust from my devotees' feet is smeared on my head will my headache go away." Nārada balked; he could not even contemplate the prospect of doing something so blasphemous! But the gōpīs did not think twice. They immediately gathered the dust from their feet and generously smeared the Lord's head with it. They did not care about the consequences of their seemingly sacrilegious act. As far as they were concerned, easing their Lord from pain was paramount. They were willing to suffer any consequence for this. When he saw this, Nārada realized the greatness of the gōpīs' love for the Lord.

The verse from the *Śrīmad Bhāgavatam* eloquently describes how enslaved the Lord is by devotion. Vinōbā Bhāvē mentions in *Bhāgavata Mīmāmsā*, his critical commentary on the *Bhāgavatam*, that Saint Ēknāth, one of the greatest bhaktas of Mahārāṣtra, India, gave much importance to this particular verse.

The Lord declares, "*yē bhajanti tu mām bhaktyā mayi tē tēṣu cāpyaham*" – "Those who worship me with devotion are in me and I am also in them" (*Bhagavad Gītā*, 9.29).

According to the *Śrīmad Bhāgavatam*, a devotee can approach the Lord in one of nine ways (*nava-vidha-bhakti*), depending on his predisposition:

> *śravaṇam kīrtanam viṣṇōh smaraṇam pādasēvanam*
> *arcanam vandanam dāsyam sakhyam ātmanivēdanam*
> Hearing Lord's glory, chanting the Lord's name, remembering the Lord and His divine play, serving the Lord's feet, worshipping Him, prostrating to the Lord, becoming His servant, becoming His friend, and surrendering wholly to the Lord. (7.5.23)

Hindu lore abounds with examples of each of the nine orientations. For example, Parīkṣit exemplifies *śravaṇam* (listening to the Lord's names). Śuka's way was that of *kīrtanam* (singing the glories of the Lord). Prahḷāda, who delineated the nine devotional attitudes, gained deliverance both from the torments of his father and the latter's henchmen as well as from samsāra by constant remembrance of the Lord (*smaraṇam*). Goddess Lakṣmī's unswerving devotion to Lord Viṣṇu's holy feet is an ideal example of *pādasēvanam*. When it comes to *arcanam* (constantly worshipping the Lord), King Pṛthu is the best example. Queen Kuntī offers an ideal example of *vandanam*, a reverential attitude towards God. The most beloved role model for *dāsyam* (the attitude of a servant towards the Lord) is Hanumān. Arjuna exemplifies the devotee who considers the Lord his friend and companion (*sakhyam*), and Mahābali was the very personification of *ātmanivēdanam* (complete surrender).

Some scholars are of the opinion that the Vēdas do not sanction bhakti, but this is not true. The source of all sādhana is the Vēdas, which unequivocally proclaim the glory of bhakti. The Vēdas contain hymns galore in praise of the divine. In the Vēdas, we come across ṛṣis worshipping various deities. For instance, there is a verse that extols Lord Viṣṇu thus: "Whoever worships Viṣṇu conquers and wins over the whole universe."

We may wonder why. In his commentary on the *Viṣṇu Sahasranāma*, Śankarācārya Swāmi defines 'Viṣṇu' thus: '*vēvēṣṭi vyāpnōtīti viṣṇuḥ*' – 'Viṣṇu is the one who is all-pervading.' One who worships the all-pervading discovers the divine consciousness within oneself, too. The *haviss* (rice offering) to Viṣṇu symbolizes the offering of our vāsanās, both good and bad. Viṣṇu is also hailed as '*Purāṇa puruṣaḥ*,' i.e. one who is most ancient, yet ever fresh and new. In His presence, we never feel jaded. Isn't this how it is with Amma? No matter how long we sit near Her, we never become bored. This is because, like Viṣṇu, Amma is ever new and ever fresh. This is the uniqueness of divine wisdom. One who manifests it wins over the world. That is why Amma always says that the whole universe will bow down before a true bhakta.

Some ask if there is a place for scholarship in bhakti. The story of Pūntānam and Mēlpattūr sheds some light on this issue. Mēlpattūr Nārāyaṇa Bhaṭṭatiri was an erudite scholar who composed the *Nārāyaṇīyam*, a Sānskṛt poem that summarizes the *Bhāgavata Purāṇa*. After he had completed his composition, he was cured of rheumatism. Consequently, he became a little proud, thinking that there was no greater scholar than him.

Pūntānam Nambūtiri, a contemporary poet, was also a great devotee of Guruvāyūrappan, a manifestation of Lord Viṣṇu enshrined in the Guruvāyūr temple in Kērala. Unlike Mēlpattūr, Pūntānam composed in the vernacular (Malayāḷam), which Mēlpattūr disdained. So, when Pūntānam humbly approached Mēlpattūr and asked him to check his work, *Jñānappāna* ('Song of Wisdom'), Mēlpattūr scoffed at the suggestion and refused to do so. This rebuff hurt Pūntānam deeply. As a result, Mēlpattūr became afflicted once again with rheumatism. When he supplicated Lord Guruvāyūrappan for divine intervention in healing the disease, he heard an ethereal voice that said, "Pūntānam's *bhakti* (devotion) is more pleasing to Me than your *vibhakti* (scholarship)."

Actually, a true scholar is a true bhakta. In his commentary on the *Bhagavad Gītā*, Śankarācārya Swāmi defines punditry thus: '*paṇḍā ātmaviṣayā buddhiḥ yēṣām tē hi paṇḍitāḥ*' – '*paṇḍā* means knowledge of the Self; those indeed who have this are *paṇḍitāḥ*' (2.11).

In fact, many pundits give bhakti an elevated place, considering it the tenth *rasa* and the fifth *puruṣārtha*. In Indian art forms and poetry, there is mention of the *navarasas*, the nine aesthetic sentiments that are considered pure emotions. Similarly, Hindu scriptures talk about the four goals of life. The fact that scholars consider bhakti vitally important in both the artistic and spiritual spheres speaks of its inestimable value. For those who know it, bhakti is not something that leads to jñāna. In fact, they consider *parā-bhakti* (supreme devotion) far greater than jñāna.

In a similar vein, Amma speaks about *tattvattile bhakti*, devotion based on an understanding of spiritual principles instead of being motivated by desire (*kāmya bhakti*). She says, "Tattvattile bhakti is selflessly loving and taking refuge in God who has become everything, without thinking that there are many gods." On another occasion, Amma quipped, "Tattva bhakti embraces jñāna tightly." Truly, bhakti and jñāna are not two. Jñāna without bhakti is dry, and bhakti without jñāna is blind.

Ultimately, devotion is not something to be talked about, but experienced. One cannot understand the nature of bhakti either by learning or from lectures. As Sage Nārada says in the *Nārada Bhakti Sūtras*, "*anirvacanīyam prēmasvarūpam*" – "the nature of supreme love is beyond description" (51). It can only be understood through experience. Sage Nārada explains this further in the next aphorism: '*mūkāsvādanavat*' – 'It is like the experience of a dumb person' (52), who cannot explain the experience he has had of a tasty delicacy. Similar is the experience of one who has sipped the nectar of bhakti, after which, "*Yat jñātvā mattō bhavati, stabdhō bhavati, ātmārāmō bhavati*" – "the devotee becomes like an intoxicated person, becomes stunned, and finds all joy in his own Self" (6).

It must be remembered that one can have bhakti only with divine grace, with God's compassion. His grace and compassion are constantly flowing towards us. However, we should become worthy of receiving and containing it. What this means is that we should acquire mental purity. The *Bhāgavata Purāṇa* says that one can transmute all emotions, even *kāma* (lust) and *krōdha* (anger), into love for the divine if we offer them to God. When offered at His shrine, they become like cooked or fried seeds, which can never bear fruit.

Take the case of Kamsa, who constantly brooded on the Lord with hatred and anger. Through this obsession, Kṛṣṇa became the center of all his activities, paving the way to the blissful union with the Lord, who killed him. Pūtana, who tried to kill the Lord by smearing poison on her breasts and then feeding Him, attained salvation when the Lord slew her. The gōpīs who directed all their passions towards Kṛṣṇa became one with Him. The key is constantly remembering Him, whatever be the nature of our remembrance. If we can make our minds dwell constantly on God, His grace and compassion will undoubtedly flow into us.

9
"How do the wise sit, speak and walk?"

How do we know if someone is spiritually elevated? Admittedly, it is hard to gauge a person's spiritual standing with the yardstick of our own limited spiritual maturity. However, there is an acid test of spiritual greatness: do we feel uncommon bliss in the presence of that person? If we do, even when he or she does not look at or speak to us, then we can be sure that we are in the sacred presence of holiness.

Familiarity generally breeds contempt, but not with mahātmās. (It may be argued that they can never become familiar, so unfathomable and multifaceted is their divine being.) Every moment in their presence is uniquely joyful. Time has not diminished my bewitchment with the sheer beauty of Amma's gaze, the sweetness of Her smile, and the magnetism of Her actions. Her being is so transparent that one can clearly perceive in Her the perennial freshness of *caitanya*, divine consciousness.

Notwithstanding their appeal, mahātmās prefer to hide their spiritual light under a bushel because they are not interested in name or fame. Devoid of ego, they do not wish to exhibit their greatness. They invariably lack body-consciousness because they identify with the luminous inner core rather than the outer shell of name and form.

The life of Sadāśiva Brahmēndra is a glowing illustration of how elevated divine consciousness can be. This 18th century saint, composer and philosopher would wander around naked or semi-naked, often in an intoxicated trance.

Once, he walked through a harem of Muslim women. The harem was part of a Nawāb's home. When someone reported to him that a naked Hindu monk had just sauntered through the harem, the Nawāb went after him. Affronted by the sanyāsī's cool demeanor, he cruelly lopped off one of His arms. Sadāśiva Brahmēndra walked on as if nothing had happened. Seeing this, the Nawāb realized that He was no ordinary soul. Picking up His chopped arm, he ran after and begged forgiveness of the mahātmā. Sadāśiva Brahmēndra listened to the Nawāb, took the amputated limb, reattached it to His torso, and walked away, unfazed. It is hard to imagine a more graphic illustration of utter detachment from body-consciousness, or a more potent demonstration of spiritual presence and mastery over matter.

We might contend that such absolute disregard for the body is not possible for us. Such may be the case, but we can try to rise above our bodily limitations. Take the case of Bhīṣma, for example, a well-loved character from the *Mahābhārata*. Amma often cites him as a paragon of strength and surrender to the divine. His earthly sojourn was one long penance. He took an oath of lifelong celibacy so that his father, King Śantanu, could marry the fisherwoman Satyavatī, whose father had stipulated that his daughter's children should be the rulers. He, thus, denied himself the pleasures of both a royal and conjugal life. Pleased with his son's deference, Śantanu gave him the boon of being able to choose his moment of death. Bhīṣma was also a staunch adherent of dharma, from which he never deviated in life and death. He met a gruesome end in the battlefield of Kurukṣētra, where he was felled by a shower of arrows from Arjuna's bow. It is said that he lay on that bed of arrows for months, without his body touching the ground at all. This was possibly the worst crucifixion in history, and yet, instead of bemoaning his fate or railing against the ways of God, he serenely bore his lot, his devotion to Lord Kṛṣṇa undimmed. He chose not to end his suffering because he wanted to wait for the astrologically auspicious time when his soul would merge with the Lord, which it eventually did.

By unswervingly worshipping Kṛṣṇa and adhering to the noble virtues of truth and chastity, Bhīṣma became a hero in his own right. This is the culmination of hero worship. Everyone has a role model. For many, it is a celebrity – a Hollywood or Bollywood star, for example. For others, it might be a parent or a teacher. It is natural to look up to and emulate someone whom we think is better or greater than we are. But we should choose a role model carefully.

The renowned mythologist Joseph Campbell has said that the celebrity lives only for his or her ego, whereas the hero acts to redeem society. Kṛṣṇa was one such hero.

It was not only Bhīṣma who hero-worshipped Him. Arjuna did, too. For him, Kṛṣṇa was first a best friend and trusted ally. Later, his veneration increased to the point that the Lord became his Guru. It is at this decisive juncture that Arjuna surrendered to the supreme, universal hero, and requested Him to describe the concept of the *sthita-prajñā*, a person of steady wisdom. He asks the Lord,

> *sthitaprajñasya kā bhāṣā samādhistasya kēśava*
> *sthitadhīḥ kim prabhāṣēta kimāsīta vrajēta kim*
> What, O Kēśava, is the description of him who has steady wisdom and who is merged in the super-conscious state? How does one of steady wisdom speak? How does he sit? How does he walk?
> (*Bhagavad Gītā*, 2.54)

In outlining the characteristic attitudes of a saint established in the Self, Kṛṣṇa clearly shows that they are all attainable through effort. The first and foremost attribute is that a saint has cast off all desires and revels in the bliss of the Self. For a baby, its mother's bosom is the source of joy and security. This source is later relocated to toys. In school, the child finds happiness in the company of friends. As a teenager, he or she might find fulfillment in the latest gadgets, and in youth, in the company of the opposite sex. The search for happiness does not stop after marriage. One then strives to forge a well-paying career, and then to raise a family. In old age, one seeks support from children and the revitalizing company of grandchildren. The history of happiness is nothing but an elusive search through external objects.

The wise realize that this is a wild goose chase, and turn their attention within, wherein they find true, undying bliss. Calm and composed, their minds remain steady in pleasure and pain, and are free from attachment, fear and anger. No calamity can distress them, whether it be of a spiritual origin (*ādhyātmika*), a problem caused by something external (*ādhibhautika*), or one arising from unseen causes (*ādhidaivika*). Possessed of an unruffled demeanor, they face life's challenges undauntedly and with inner detachment. They neither rejoice in favorable circumstances nor recoil in adverse ones. Just as a tortoise draws in its limbs, they withdraw their senses from sense-objects. In any case, having realized God, they no longer have a taste for sense pleasures.

We are blessed to be contemporaries of Amma, who has become the role model of many all over the world. She is a veritable treasury of many sterling qualities. To assimilate fully just one of those qualities is a lifetime's work for most. Adoration of the right role model thus becomes a means to fulfilling our own spiritual potential.

Amma's definition of heroism is very similar to what is expressed in the *Bhagavad Gītā*. As She memorably says, in order to be a hero, one should become a zero. In denying oneself, one fulfills one's spiritual potential. When we become nothing, we become everything. This is the promise of self-abnegation.

Carl Jung, founder of analytical psychology, once said that the purpose of life was to relocate the center of the personality from the ego to the Self. For mahātmās, their center has always been the Self. They do not identify with their bodies, and attribute all sense of 'doer-ship' to God.

To defer to God in all things is not a weakness. To attribute agency to Him does not disempower us; rather, it empowers us in ways we could never imagine possible. Instead of relying on our puny muscles, we can flex cosmic muscles. The best illustration of such deference was Hanumān, devotee par excellence of Lord Rāma. Hanumān's exploits are legendary. In a literal leap of faith, he bounded across the Indian Ocean to land in Śrī Lanka, where he was instrumental in rescuing Sītā, his Lord's consort, and in destroying the capital of Rāma's arch-enemy, Rāvaṇa. Through his devotion to Lord Rāma, he literally moved the Ṛṣabhādri Mountain from its Himālayan abode to Lanka, where he was able to revive Lakṣmaṇa, Rāma's brother, and other fallen soldiers in Rāma's camp with its life-giving herb, the *mṛtasañjīvanī.*

What was the secret behind his superhuman prowess? The name of the Lord. Hanumān had total faith in the potency of this divine name. Every atom in his body reverberated with the word 'Rāma.' For Hanumān, 'Rāma' was not just a name; it was a mantra, the most potent incantation that allowed him to achieve the impossible. He believed with all his heart that his body was merely the conduit for the divine energy of his beloved Master. Hanumān was as genuinely humble as he was formidably strong. Through self-surrender, he conquered the heart of Śrī Rāma, and became the touchstone of undying devotion.

We can also cultivate the idea that we are merely instruments in the hands of God. Consider a pencil: it can write the most beautiful script only if it is in the hands of a master playwright. It will be sharpened periodically, but this pain makes it a better instrument. If it errs, it will be able to correct the mistake with its eraser. A pencil is not defined by its color or shape, but by what is inside it, i.e. the lead. No matter how challenging the situation, if it continues to write, it will make a mark in the world.

Similarly, each one of us can do great things, but only if we humbly allow God to take us into His hands. Put another way, it is better to write the script of our lives with a pencil, and to let God script our destinies with a pen. In His infallibility, He will do what is best for us.

At present, we are possessed by the niggling sense of 'doer-ship.' An analogy will reveal how deluded we are. When melted by the sun's rays, the snow on the mountains becomes water, which flows as a river. The river reflects the sun, which, together with gravity, is responsible for making it flow towards the ocean. How foolish it would be if the river imagined that it were flowing of its own accord. Similarly, what enlivens us is the sun of divine consciousness – the same divine consciousness that sleeps in minerals, moves in plants and animals in varying degrees, and expresses itself as awareness in human beings. This gift of mindfulness is imbued only in humans, and if we fail to recognize and honor it, we will have missed the opportunity to fulfill our purpose in life.

Suppose there are different pots of water. The sun is reflected in each one of them, but this does not mean that there are many suns. Similarly, the sun of divinity shines in each one of us as consciousness. It is this vision of oneness, i.e. the ability to see the common denominator amongst varied forms, which distinguishes the enlightened ones from others. Mahātmās do not harbor the illusory sense of difference, and it is because they see themselves in others that they are able to draw others spontaneously, like iron filings to a magnet.

Individuality is an illusion, the mistaken notion that we are different from God. Our sense of difference is superficial. We look different, and so we think we are different. We think differently, and thus take pride in ideological differences. But our essential self lies behind these different names and forms. This essence existed before we were named or before we could even think. It is the bedrock of our existence.

Emerson, the noted American essayist, lecturer and poet, once said that, "Every man is God playing the fool." The foolishness is fostered by the illusion of free will. Do we really have free will? Does a ball thrown upwards have free will? All our actions are prompted by our vāsanās. Vāsanās determine the direction our actions are likely to take. Someone who is quick-tempered is likely to respond differently to a situation from someone without that tendency. Thus, our actions are colored by our previous conditioning. Similarly, the karmic balance we have inherited from previous births determine how much 'purchasing power' we have in this life. Those saddled with a heavy karmic debt will, perforce, find themselves in onerous situations, whereas those who are born with a healthy balance of meritorious deeds from previous lives will encounter more conducive circumstances. The sole purpose of spirituality is the removal of vāsanās. For this, the guidance of a spiritual master is essential.

Nevertheless, we are the architects of our own destiny. By doing good deeds in the present, we can pave a better future for ourselves. By practicing self-control, we can slowly wear away negative vāsanās. Sanātana Dharma upholds the power of self-effort to counteract destiny. What we start with is less important than how we finish. This implies striving.

A girl, the 20th of 22 children, was born prematurely and her survival was doubtful. When she was four, the polio virus paralyzed her left leg. She then had to wear a brace, which deformed that leg. When she was nine, she removed the metal leg brace she had been dependent on and began to walk without it. But she still had to wear an orthopedic shoe to support the foot. Over the next few years, she was also afflicted by bouts of polio and scarlet fever. When she turned 12, she stopped wearing the special orthopedic shoe, thus achieving her dream of becoming like other children. That year, this girl decided to become a runner. She entered a race and came in last. For the next few years, she was the last in every race she entered. Many told her to quit, but she persevered. One day, she won a race and then another. From then on, she won every race she entered. Eventually, the little girl, Wilma Rudolph, went on to win three track-and-field gold medals in the 1960 Olympics.

Her life is a triumph of nurture over nature. Destiny is not necessarily carved in stone. Our role in life unfolds according to an open-ended script that we have freedom to change through our actions and determinations. In His beneficence, God dispenses our karma in such a way as not only to exhaust our prārabdha but also elevate us. The law of karma might seem severe and exacting, but it is tempered with compassion. The Creator knows, more than we do, what each being in His creation needs, and always acts infallibly. A well-known poem expresses the paradoxical ways of the Lord:

When I asked God for strength,
He gave me difficult situations to face.
When I asked God for brains and brawn,
He gave me puzzles to solve.
When I asked God for happiness,
He showed me some unhappy people.
When I asked God for wealth,
He showed me how to work hard.
When I asked God for favors,

He showed me opportunities to work hard.
When I asked God for peace,
He showed me how to help others.
God gave me nothing I wanted –
He gave me everything I needed.

The war-time experiences of Victor Frankl, a psychiatrist who was imprisoned in Auschwitz, Dachau and other concentration camps during World War II, were harrowing, to say the least. His father, mother, brother and wife died in gas ovens, and he was treated like a beast of burden, all the while exposed to freezing cold, severe hunger and other cruel deprivations. Under the unrelenting pressure of extreme trauma that lasted a few years, Frankl discovered meaning in his suffering, and thus found a reason to continue living. His experiences bore out the truth of the dictum made famous by Friedrich Wilhelm Nietzsche, the well-known existentialist: "He who has a *why* to live can bear with almost any *how*."

Frankl describes a day when he was overcome by pain (from foot sores caused by wearing torn shoes and walking many kilometers daily), worries about whether he would get enough food that day, and anxieties about the brutal guards he might have to face. When he realized how he was allowing his mind to be caught up in this turmoil, he was able to create a distance between himself and his thoughts and emotions. Using imagination as a creative tool, Frankl imagined himself giving a lecture on the psychology of the concentration camp to a rapt audience in a well-lit, warm and pleasant lecture theater. He says, "By this method I succeeded somehow in rising above the situation, above the sufferings of the moment, and I observed them as if they were already of the past. Both I and my troubles became the object of an interesting psychoscientific study undertaken by myself." What Frankl is describing here is nothing other than witnessing the situations in life.

Frankl observed first-hand that people had an inner capacity to overcome apathy and suppress irritation, no matter what the circumstance. Even in the dire straits of imprisonment, starvation and physical torture during the war, he noted that one might be robbed of everything except "the last of the human freedoms – to choose one's attitude in any given set of circumstances, to choose one's way." Difficult situations offer opportunities either to forgo one's dignity and betray one's lower, animalistic tendencies of selfishness and cruelty, or to allow one to summon the inner reserves of selflessness and dignity. He describes how one of his guards secretly gave him a piece of bread, which he had saved from his own breakfast ration.

At other times, during forced marches on slippery ice, when sheer fatigue was about to overwhelm the prisoners, Frankl would resort to visualizing the face of his beloved wife with "uncanny acuteness. I heard her answering me, saw her smile, her frank and encouraging look. Real or not, her look was then more luminous than the sun." He then reflected, "I understood how man who has nothing left in the world still may know bliss... in the contemplation of his beloved. In a position of utter desolation... when his only achievement may consist in enduring his sufferings... man can, through loving contemplation of the image he carries of his beloved, achieve fulfillment." Once again, Frankl found redemption through the healthy practice of positive thinking and the attitude of being a witness, though he may not have used those terms.

God does answer our prayers, but it may not be in the ways we expect. He expects effort on our part, and when we do our duty, His grace ensures that we are rewarded amply. We receive not just the fruits of our labor; our hearts become more expansive as a result of growing kinship with others. Ultimately, God wants all of us to realize our true, divine essence. All the spiritual practices that Amma and other Masters have enjoined upon us will bring us closer to God; Their word is our unfailing guarantee.

The Self-realized already possess the qualities that Kṛṣṇa enumerated when discoursing on the sthita-prajñā – *viz.* desirelessness, detachment, imperturbability, equanimity on encountering the good or bad, and withdrawal of sense organs from sense objects. We must strive to earn these traits through effort. In this sense, every seeker is a work in spiritual progress, whatever his or her level of spiritual attainment.

Although self-effort is valid currency in the world of spirituality, what yields the highest dividends is divine grace. It is like the imprint on the coin, which determines its value. We must unfurl the sail of self-effort, but ultimately, it is the wind of divine grace that will help us make spiritual progress.

Epilogue:
"Are you faithful?"

Once, a man who had been on a long journey in a forest stopped to rest below a shady tree. He did not know that the tree was a *kalpa-vṛkṣa*, a magical wish-fulfilling tree. He was overwhelmed by hunger and exhaustion, not having eaten for three days. He thought, "If only I could get some delicious food now!" No sooner had the thought arisen in his mind than a delectable feast appeared before his very eyes. He did not spend too much time pondering the wheres and hows of this miracle. He just ate to his heart's content. When he had finished, he was overcome by a pleasurable languor, and another thought spontaneously arose in his mind: if only I had a nice bed to sleep on. Presto! A huge bed covered with soft linen and downy pillows appeared right in front of him. Grinning from ear to ear, he sank into the luxurious bed.

Within moments, his vāsanās started rearing their heads. The thought of *apsaras*, heavenly beauties, arose in his mind, and he thought, "If I had some of them here, life would be perfect!" Lo and behold, he found himself in bed with celestial damsels of exquisite beauty. What more could he ask for? He was beside himself with happiness.

Suddenly, a doubt arose in his mind, "What if a tiger appears and attacks me?" That was the end of the man!

God or the Guru is also a kalpa-vṛkṣa. When we have taken refuge at the shady tree of dharma, we should make the most of the rare opportunity to elevate ourselves spiritually. We have the power of discretion to choose between *śrēyas* and *prēyas*, the good and the pleasant. The choice is ours. Let us choose wisely.

According to the Hindu scriptures, the goal of life is *samādhi*, wherein the mind becomes established in the Truth. It is a state of complete desirelessness. The goal of life is perfect poise of mind. This is just what Amma silently proclaimed at birth.

The silence of samādhi is not a void, but a womb of infinite potential. The story of how Vēda Vyāsa came to compose the *Bhāgavata Purāṇa* is illustrative.

One day, Vyāsa was sitting in solitude by the bank of a river. Unexpectedly, Sage Nārada appeared before him. Vyāsa received Him with all due reverence, and the two saints started conversing. At one point, Vyāsa said, "Though I have compiled the four *Vēdas* and authored many *Purāṇas*, the *Brahmasūtram* and the *Mahābhārata*, I am still dissatisfied. O Nārada, kindly tell me why this is so?"

Nārada replied, "Your works are truly immortal. Now, through one-pointed concentration, recollect the glories of Śrī Kṛṣṇa, compose your magnum opus, and gain everlasting contentment."

This state of one-pointedness and silence is an all-inclusive state wherein one's limited individuality has expanded to include everything. At present, our life is a continuous flow of experiences. If we can understand and analyze one experience properly, we can understand the whole of life.

Every experience is constituted of the experiencer, the experienced and the experience. The experiencer, the 'I' or subject who experiences everything, is the fundamental constituent. The second constituent, the experienced, refers to the object or the world. The third constituent, the experience, is the connecting link between the two. Most tend to focus on the second and third constituents instead of the primary dimension of life (experiencer), though it is the only one with us all the time. We say things like, "I saw a beautiful mountain," "I had vivid dreams" or "I slept well." Such statements reveal the fundamental separation between 'I' and the experience. We barely realize this distinction because the 'I' has become darkly obscured by the mind. By becoming identified with the mind, which is thickly granulated by vāsanās and extroversion, we become enslaved by its dictates.

Most people are so extroverted that they lack awareness. The irony is that for all their knowledge, they are not conscious of the divine consciousness that enlivens and animates them. Amma narrates the story of how God came to dwell within the heart of man.

God created earth so that He could give Himself a place to live. That is why He made the earth beautiful, with trees and plants, animals and birds, mountains and valleys, seas and rivers. Everything was perfect. After many years of living blissfully, God decided to create human beings. As soon as that thought arose, humans came into being. And from that day onwards, there was no peace for Him!

Human beings started complaining to God day and night. They would knock on His door even in the middle of the night. God soon lost His peace of mind. No matter what He did, people would complain. When He brought forth rain in response to the farmer who complained about the drought, the potter would complain to Him about the lack of sunshine. Nobody wanted to die, but the coffin makers wanted people to die all the time.

God asked His advisors what to do. Some advised Him to go to the Himālayas, but in His omniscience, God knew that Hillary and the Sherpas, followed by other mountaineers, would scale the Everest soon. When other advisors suggested that God shift to the moon, God said that Neil Armstrong was already on his way there.

There was silence. After some time, an elderly man known for his wisdom walked up to God and whispered something in His ear. God's face brightened and He began grinning. "Wonderful!" He exclaimed.

What had the old man told God? "Hide deep within man. He will never think of looking for God there!"

One of the mantras in Amma's *Aṣṭōttaram* is *'ōm antar-mukha svabhāvāyai namaḥ'* – 'Salutations to Amma, who is, by nature, inwardly drawn' (5). Her gaze is turned within, as it were, because bliss lies within, not in the empirical realm of sense objects. As we chant the *Aṣṭōttaram* daily, let us remind ourselves to become more introspective.

Meditation is a state of the mind, rather than a process. All attempts at meditating are, as Amma says, only steps taken to reach the state of real meditation. When it comes to meditation, we should not make the mistake of restricting our efforts only to the time between sitting down on our *āsana*, our meditation seat, and getting up from it. Every action should be a preparation. Gradually, the mind slips into a meditative state, and one who becomes established in it, remains still within, even amidst a whirlwind of external activity. Such a person has an acutely heightened awareness.

There was a sage named 'Akṣapāda.' *'Akṣa'* means 'eye' and *'pāda'* means foot. To have 'eyes on one's feet' means that he was very watchful of his every move. He was aware of each and every step he took. Such awareness is the goal of spirituality.

At every step towards the goal, we have to practice negation: 'not this, not this.' In Sānskṛt, this is called *vyatirēka* (negation). The opposite of vyatirēka is *anvaya* (affirmation). When one has reached the non-dual state, one is able to reconcile and integrate all the disparate experiences of life in the vastness of Self-realization. If we observe Amma, we can intuit this transcendental state in Her. She receives everyone who comes to Her with tireless love and compassion, and accepts every situation with complete attention. Amidst the unceasing swirl of the world, Amma remains anchored to the non-dual Self. Perhaps, there can be no better example today of someone who lives in the world but is not of the world.

The Guru is someone who takes one to this ultimate purpose of life, and that is why He is placed on the highest pedestal in Indian culture. The *Guru Gītā* extols the Preceptor thus:

> *anēka janma samprāptaḥ karma bandha vidāhinē*
> *ātmajñāna pradānēna tasmai śrī guravē namaḥ*
> Salutations to the Guru, who, by imparting Self-knowledge, burns up all the karmas accumulated over countless lifetimes. (73)

The Guru being *nitya-mukta*, ever-free, is able to remove all the bonds of the disciple's karmas and confer spiritual liberation. Truly, the greatness and glory of the Guru cannot be adequately expressed. He is unlike other teachers. An ordinary teacher is, for all his learning, still ignorant of the Self, whereas the Guru is wise, for He knows the Self, and, therefore, the Self of all. A teacher teaches by words and precepts, whereas the Guru imparts through silence and by example. A teacher refers to textbooks, a Guru, to the book of personal experience. A teacher feeds the student with information; a Guru empties the disciple's head of its foolishness. A teacher shows the student how to be smart; a Guru teaches one how to be humble. A teacher will feel hurt if the student does not show him respect. A Guru is hurt when the disciple shows disrespect to anyone. A teacher expects to receive from the pupil, whereas a Guru gives with no expectation of return. A teacher is a transient phase in the student's life, whereas a Guru remains with the *śiṣya* for lifetimes until the disciple becomes illumined.

How can we ever repay Amma for what She has done and is doing? We cannot. However, we can try to cultivate two important qualities: faith and loyalty. Faith is not something that we can acquire intellectually. It is a heartfelt conviction. The following story illustrates the nature of faith.

A scholar was giving a discourse on the power of God's names. He said, "The name of God is the ship that allows one to cross the ocean of samsāra, as if the ocean were merely a small puddle." A few village milkmaids who were passing that way heard these words of the scholar and took them to heart. They thought, "Why pay one rupee to the boatman daily when we can cross the river by chanting the Lord's name?" Simple was their faith, but strong, too. The next day, they started chanting "Rāma" and thus waded across the river to the other side to sell milk.

To express their appreciation to the scholar, one of the milkmaids invited him home for dinner, and he agreed. When they reached the riverbank, the pundit paused while the milkmaid just walked across, chanting "Rāma." When she reached the far side and saw that the preacher had still not crossed the river, she walked back to ask him what the problem was. The pundit, stunned by what he had seen the milkmaid do, replied that he was waiting for the boatman. When she told him to chant "Rāma" and follow her, he hesitated. Then, he took a long rope, tied it around his waist, gave one end of it to the milkmaid, and asked her to go across with it and hold on to it tightly. When she had done so, the scholar started chanting "Rāma" rather feebly and began walking into the waters. Not surprisingly, he did not stay afloat.

Unlike the Goddess who remains afloat on the lotus, the scholar *did* have an ego, and unlike the milkmaid, he did *not* have faith. And that is why he sank.

Another moving tale of faith can be found in the annals of the Christian crusades. When the Christians were losing the war in Jerusalem, an old warrior told the other soldiers about a dream he had had: the archangel Gabriel had appeared to him and told him that a spear Jesus Christ had touched was buried here, and that if the crusaders could find it, they would win the battle. When they heard this, all the soldiers began digging at once. After hours of excavation, they found an old, rusty spear, which they assumed was the one Jesus had touched. They then resumed fighting with renewed vigor and soon won the battle.

At the time of his death, the old warrior confessed to his priest that he had made up the story about the spear in order to boost the morale of his fellow soldiers so that they could win the holy war in Jerusalem. What is significant here is not the lie, but the strength that faith had infused in the men.

Doggedness is a quality of loyalty. Like the mutt that adhered to Yudhiṣṭhira as he slowly made his way to heaven, a true disciple sticks to the Guru through thick and thin. The path to God will not always be strewn with rose petals, but if we remain with Amma, we will be amply recompensed with the ultimate benediction.

Once, when Amma visited a devotee's house, She was received with utmost devotion by the devotee, an elderly woman. She kept calling Amma "Kṛṣṇa!" and plied Her with many things to eat. Her behavior reminded me of the story of how Vidura's wife, who, like her husband, was an ardent devotee of the Lord, received Kṛṣṇa. In a state of crazed devotion, she unpeeled the bananas that she intended to offer the Lord, threw the bananas away, and offered the peels to the Lord! Kṛṣṇa accepted the peels with relish because He saw the love behind the offering rather than the offering itself. Similarly, Amma looked very pleased with the loving ministrations of this devotee.

After some time, She went to the *pūja* room (where ceremonial worship is done). There was only one idol there: that of Lord Kṛṣṇa. The devotee had adorned it so beautifully that the idol looked alive. Amma told her that Kṛṣṇa always tests His devotees by giving them some suffering, which was His way of strengthening their devotion, and then asked her if she intended to worship only Kṛṣṇa. Amma suggested that the devotee place idols or images of other deities as well on the altar. The devotee refused point-blank. She said that Kṛṣṇa was the only God she knew and that she had complete faith in Him. Even though she saw Amma as Her Guru, it was only because she was convinced that Amma was no different from Kṛṣṇa. Yet the form of Kṛṣṇa was so captivating to her that she did not want to worship any other form.

When Amma heard her answer, She looked pleased. Actually, She had been testing the devotee's *ananya bhakti*, exclusive devotion to one form. The gōpīs of Vṛndāvan are hailed even today for their all-consuming passion for the Lord, devotion that culminated in their becoming wholly saturated with Kṛṣṇa-consciousness.

After I had recorded *'Śrī Rāmacandra Kṛpālu'* around 2002, I sensed my life-long devotion to Lord Kṛṣṇa, my iṣṭa dēva, shifting to Lord Rāma. I could not understand why. During this phase, I kept ruminating on the latter's life.

Lord Rāma, hailed as *maryādā puruṣōttama*, was the very epitome of dharma. The word 'maryādā' refers to the finest and noblest conduct. The term 'puruṣōttama' means 'the best among men.' Taken together, the epithet means that Rāma was adjudged the best among men for His unswerving dedication to truth and dharma. No true saint ever deviates from dharma, but from the limited understanding that a human perspective offers, some of his actions might *seem* questionable. Even so, the probity of Rāma's actions is less likely to be called into question compared with the actions of Kṛṣṇa.

Further, His renowned devotee and disciple, Hanumān, is considered a partial incarnation of Rudra, i.e. Lord Śiva Himself, one of the Holy Trinity. To me, this meant that Lord Śiva Himself wanted to serve Rāma in Hanumān's form. It is said that Lord Śiva is ever engaged in chanting Rāma's name, and that He advised His consort, Śrī Pārvatī, with a Rāma mantra. He declared,

> *śrī rāma rāma rāmēti*
> *ramē rāmē manōramē*
> *sahasra nāma tattulyam*
> *rāma nāma varānanē*
>
> O Varānanā (lovely-faced woman), I chant the holy name of Rāma again and again, and thus constantly enjoy this beautiful sound. This holy name of Rāmacandra is equal to one thousand holy names of Lord Viṣṇu. (*Viṣṇu-sahasranāma-stōtram*)

These thoughts preoccupied my mind for a period of time, and for the first time in my life, I felt that the foremost among divinities was Lord Rāma; none other compared to Him. He was ideal in every respect: a filial son, a loving brother, a faithful husband, a loyal friend, a righteous ruler, and a staunch defender of dharma. I never confided my thoughts in anyone, not even Amma.

During this phase, after spending a few days in Amṛtapuri, I returned to Pālakkāṭ. It was a Tuesday, the day when Amma serves prasād lunch to āśram residents. Late in the afternoon, a brahmacārī called me and said that Amma had been talking about me during Her satsang. I was curious to know what She had said. He said that Amma was talking about what an ardent devotee of Kṛṣṇa I was, and how I had cried inconsolably when She stopped Her Kṛṣṇa Bhāva darśan in the olden days. And then, She had added, "I wonder whether he is thinking of changing his iṣṭa-dēvatā now."

Without my uttering even a word to Amma, She had intuited the direction the stream of my thoughts was taking me.

Some weeks later, when I came to Amṛtapuri, I went to Amma's room. She spoke on various spiritual topics, eventually settling on the topic of death. Amma said, "How fleeting life is! A person who is here today is gone tomorrow. Such is the ultimate destiny of all beings." She further said that the ego or mind was death; one who overcomes the ego or mind overcomes death. Amma said that 'one who dies while living' does not die. Paradoxical as it sounds, what Amma meant was that one who has died to physical existence (i.e. been born to spiritual existence) will never ever experience annihilation for he is attuned to pure and eternal spiritual experience. As the Buddha remarked, "Even death is not to be feared by one who has lived wisely."

All of a sudden, Amma took a ring that was kept on a side table and slipped it on one of my fingers. When I looked at it, I was shocked to see the signet of a flute on a banyan leaf. This image is inextricably associated with Lord Kṛṣṇa. Amma did not say anything; She did not have to. I had already understood Her hint: that one should not change one's iṣṭa-dēvatā, with whom the jīvātmā has been associated by bonds of devotion over lifetimes. This experience signaled the end of my obsession with Lord Rāma and restored my native devotion to Kṛṣṇa.

We can learn the importance of loyalty from the humble honeybee. Unlike other insects that pollinate, the bee is singularly remarkable for seeking pollen from only one species of flowers, thus ensuring the proliferation of that species. Other insects are interested only in searching for pollen, with the result that many flowers remain unfertilized. Just as the bee demonstrates flower fidelity, we should be loyal to our Guru. To do so is not a sign of cultish behavior, but an expression of one-pointed love, which the scriptures uphold as a necessary ingredient for spiritual progress. As a wit pointed out, if we go to one doctor, we get a prescription; from two, confusion; and from three, cremation!

Sometimes, the Guru may show anger and seemingly turn away from us. This is when a real devotee or disciple proves his or her mettle. The story of Viṭhōba, father of the illustrious 13th century Mahārāṣtrian saint Jñānēśvar, is revealing. Although married, the dispassionate Viṭhōba had hidden this fact from his Guru Śrīpāda Swāmi and accepted sanyāsa from Him. When the Guru realized this, He rebuked him and told him to go back to his wife and to lead a householder's life. At this, Viṭhōba pleaded with his Guru. His impassioned plea is humble yet firm, a lyrical defense of loyalty and faithfulness. He says,

> O Master, I will not turn to anybody else. A chaste woman will not choose even the trinity of gods over her husband. Similarly, I will not seek refuge in anyone else. Even if the husband is a rogue, will she go in search of a respectable man? Despite his ill-repute, will she not worship him alone as her Lord? What a fate awaits a disciple who deserts his Guru, finding fault with him! Remember the fate of Triśanku who became ostracized by society for deserting, Vasiṣṭha, his Guru. I have cast my lot

> with You, and so, I will not retrace my steps or turn in any other direction. Why do you put me through these tests? Please be kind enough to destroy my ego, cut asunder the knot of ignorance, impart the knowledge of the Self and bestow on me eternal bliss.

His assertions about a chaste wife being loyal to an unprincipled husband might sound anachronistic or even foolish today. Be that as it may, Viṭhōba's overriding tone is of abiding loyalty towards one's Guru. Having devotion to one's Guru is a mark of God's grace. It is not different from having love for God, for the Guru is one with God. To feel that ardor of devotion in Amma's physical presence is relatively easy. Feeding the flame of bhakti when we are away from Her is challenging.

A portrait of true devotion is given by the Bengāli saint Caitanya Mahāprabhu, who was hailed as the incarnation of divine love. During one of His tours across India, He saw a religious program in which many people were reciting the *Bhagavad Gītā*. Among them, He saw a man shedding tears profusely. Out of sheer curiosity, Caitanya Mahāprabhu approached this man. He saw that the man was not reciting the verses. In fact, he did not even have the *Gītā* with him. He asked the man why he was not chanting with the others. The man replied, "I cannot read or understand the Sānskṛt verses, but when I hear the recitation, I see Śrī Kṛṣṇa in the battlefield of Kurukṣētra, dispensing divine wisdom to Arjuna. When I think about the infinite glory and compassion of the Lord, how can I not cry?"

As Amma has repeatedly assured Her children, "Where there is love, distance is no barrier." She cites the analogy of how the sun's rays make a lotus blossom on earth even though the sun is far away. We can take heart from this example. Even though the physical distance between Amma and us may be large, we can worship Amma or God in our hearts, Her real abode. Even though the gap between God and us may seem insuperable on account of our drawbacks, we should always remember that the Divine Mother is most merciful. The *Laḷitā Sahasranāma* says that She destroys even the greatest of sins – '*Om mahā pātaka nāśinyai namaḥ*' (214). What matters is the effort we put forth to bridge the seeming gap between Amma and ourselves. More than anything else, we should be honest with ourselves about how much we want Amma and the spiritual life.

Some years ago, while in Santa Fe, New Mexico, I was listening with great devotion to some Kṛṣṇa bhajans. One of them in particular, which described the Lord and His *līlās* (divine play), moved me so much that I became very emotional. I keenly felt the reverential love in the singer's voice, and such was the beauty of his singing that I began sobbing my heart out. When the floodgate of tears finally closed, I felt a strong urge to see Amma. It was about 6:30 p.m. I went straight to Amma's room in the Santa Fe āśram. She was about to leave for bhajans. As soon as Amma saw me, She said beamingly, "Praṇavam! What brings you here? Amma was just thinking of you."

She seemed to be in the most congenial mood. In hindsight, I felt that it must have been because I had been devoutly contemplating the glories of Lord Kṛṣṇa, and Amma, who is one with the Supreme, must have picked up on my devotional fervor. Without any preamble, I emotionally burst out, "Amma! I want a boon from You. If I have to be reborn..."

Before I could complete my sentence, Amma said, "...you will be with me! Don't worry, son, you will always be with me if you are reborn."

Amma's words made me feel greatly reassured. About two months before the publication of this book, I was in Her room. Thoughts of how glorious a Master She was, how loving, kind and compassionate completely overwhelmed me. I helplessly began sobbing. In that emotional state, I told Amma, "Lord Kṛṣṇa incarnated about 5,000 years ago, during the Dvāpara Yuga. And now, You have incarnated and are with us today. How long will it be before You grace the earth again with Your divine presence? What if I have to be reborn again soon after I die? I cannot imagine a life without You at all!" I broke down crying uncontrollably.

Gazing at me with immense compassion, Amma wiped the tears off my face. Then, taking my hands in Hers, She said emphatically, "Amma is giving You Her word that You will be reborn only when Amma comes to earth again. You will always be with Me!"

When I heard those words, with their sweet infusion of maternal love and divine confidence, I felt immensely elated. By what grace had I come under this divine wish-fulfilling tree, this kalpa-vṛkṣa?

May Amma's divine grace lead us all to the infinite effulgence of the soul.

VIMAL

glossary

abhyāsa Unrelenting (spiritual) practice.

adharma Unrighteousness. Deviation from natural harmony.

ādhibhautika Pertaining to something in the material world.

ādhidaivika Pertaining to an unseen force.

Ādi Śankarācārya Saint who is believed to have lived between the eighth and ninth centuries CE, and who is revered as a Guru and chief proponent of the *Advaita* (non-dual) philosophy.

adhyātmā Pertaining to the *ātmā*, the Self.

ādhyātmika Pertaining to something of spiritual origin.

adṛṣṭa phalam Literally, 'unseen fruit.' Refers to the unmanifested consequence of action.

Advaita Not two; non-dual; philosophy that holds that the *jīva* (individual soul) and

	jagat (universe) are ultimately one with *Brahman*, the Supreme Reality.
Agni	Fire God and presiding deity of speech.
aham	'I;' used in Vēdāntic discourses to refer to the subject of all experience; distinguished from ***idam***.
Akbar	One of the emperors of the Mogul dynasty in India who ruled from 1556 – 1605 CE.
Amma	Malayāḷam word for 'mother.'
Amṛtapuri	International headquarters of the Mātā Amṛtānandamayī Maṭh, located at Amma's birth place in Kēraḷa, India.
Ananta	'Without end' or infinite. King of the *nāgas* (serpent deities). Viṣṇu is often depicted as reclining on him. Said to hold all the planets on its hoods.
anvaya	Affirmation, concordance or agreement; connection or association; often contrasted with ***vyatirēka***.
ārati	Clockwise movement of a lamp aflame with burning camphor, to propitiate a deity, usually signifying the closing of a ceremonial worship.
arcana	Chanting of a litany of divine names.

arcanam Worshipping the Lord ; see ***nava-vidha-bhakti.***

Arjuna Third of the Pāṇḍava brothers and close companion of Kṛṣṇa.

āsana A seat, often a cloth on which a seeker meditates or does other spiritual practice; in *haṭha yōga*, a specific posture.

āśram Monastery. Amma defines it as a compound: '*ā*' – 'that' and '*śramam*' – 'effort' (toward Self-realization).

Aṣṭōttaram Litany of 108 attributes.

ātmā Self or Soul.

ātmanivēdanam Self-surrender; see ***nava-vidha-bhakti.***

aum/ōm Primordial sound in the universe; the seed of creation; the cosmic sound, which can be heard in deep meditation; the sacred mantra, taught in the Upaniṣads, which signifies Brahman, the divine ground of existence; in the meditation that Amma teaches, the sound that one mentally synchronizes with every exhalation during the initial

	stages of meditation (before the sound dissolves into the breath).
avadhūta	An enlightened person whose behavior is at odds with social norms.
avatar	Divine incarnation.
Ayōdhyā	Ancient Indian city, birthplace of Rāma, and setting of the *Rāmāyaṇa.*
Ayyappa	Hindu deity, born of the union of Śiva and Mōhinī, a female incarnation of Viṣṇu.
Bhadrakāḷī	An auspicious form of Kāḷī who protects the good; see Kāḷī.
Bhagavad Gītā	Literally, 'Song of the Lord,' it consists of 18 chapters of verses in which Lord Kṛṣṇa advises Arjuna. The advice is given on the battlefield of Kurukṣētra, just before the righteous Pāṇḍavas fight the unrighteous Kauravas. It is a practical guide to overcoming crises in one's personal or social life, and is the essence of Vēdic wisdom.
bhajan	Devotional song or hymn in praise of God.
bhakta	Devotee.

bhakti	Devotion for God.
bhakti mārga	Path of devotion.
bharaṇi	Poetic genre used for glorifying military heroes.
Bharata	Brother of Rāma.
bhāva	Divine mood; attitude.
bhāvanā	Imagination; 'calling into existence.'
Bhīṣma	Character from the *Mahābhārata*; son of King Śantanu, and granduncle of both the Pāṇḍavas and Kauravas.
bilva	*Aegle marmelos*. The leaves of this tree are sacred to Hindus.
Bīrbal	Adviser in Akbar's court, he was well-known for his wit and wisdom.
Brahmā	Lord of Creation in the Hindu Trinity.
Brahma-lōka	The world of Brahmā, the Creator.
Brahman	Ultimate Truth beyond any attributes; the Supreme Reality underlying all life; the divine ground of existence.
Brahmasthānam	Literally, 'place of Brahman.' The name of the temples Amma has consecrated in various parts of India and in Mauritius. The temple shrine features a unique four-faced idol that symbolizes the unity behind the diversity of divine forms.

Brahma Sūtram	'Aphorisms on the Ultimate Truth;' one of the three canonical texts of Vēdānta and a summary of the teachings of the Upaniṣads.
Brāhmin	One who belongs to the priestly caste. The four main castes in Indian society are *Brāhmaṇa* (priestly clan), *Kṣatriya* (martial clan), *Vaiśya* (trading community) and *Śūdra* (serving community).
Buddha	'Awakened One;' from 'budh' (to know, to wake up); a reference to Sage Gautama Buddha.
buddhi	Intellect.
caitanya	Divine consciousness.
dama	Sense control, or the control of both *jñāna indriyas* (organs of perception) and *karma indriyas* (organs of action).
darśan	Audience with a holy person or a vision of the Divine.
Daśaratha	Father of Rāma.
dāsyam	The attitude of a servant towards God; see ***nava-vidha-bhakti***.

Dēvakī	Mother of Kṛṣṇa.
Dēvī	Goddess/Divine Mother.
dharma	Literally, 'that which upholds (creation).' Generally used to refer to the harmony of the universe, a righteous code of conduct, sacred duty or eternal law.
dōśa	Indian pancake.
Draupadī	Wife of the Pāṇḍavas, also known as Pāñcālī.
Drōṇa	Also known as Drōṇācārya, he was the teacher of both the Pāṇḍavas and the Kauravas; a master of military arts.
dṛṣṭa phalam	Literally, 'visible fruit.' Refers to the perceived consequence of action.
Durvāsa	Ancient sage known for his flaming temper.
Duryōdhana	Eldest of the 100 sons of King Dhṛtarāṣṭra and Queen Gāndhārī; leader of the Kaurava clan; and claimant to the throne of Hastinapura.
Duśśāsana	A Kaurava prince, second son of King Dhṛtarāṣṭra and Queen Gāndhārī, and younger brother of Duryōdhana; infamous for attempting to disrobe Draupadī.

dvaita	Duality; the philosophy that holds that *īśvara* (God) and *jagat* (universe) are eternally separate and real. God is the only independent reality.
Dvāpara	See ***yuga***.
Dvāraka	Capital of kingdom that Kṛṣṇa established after He left Mathura.
Gōkula	Village near Mathura where Kṛṣṇa spent His childhood.
gōpa	Cowherd boy from Vṛndāvan.
gōpī	Milk maiden from Vṛndāvan. The gōpīs were known for their ardent devotion to Lord Kṛṣṇa. Their devotion exemplifies the most intense love for God.
gōpuram	Monumental tower that marks the entrance to South Indian temples.
guṇa	One of three types of qualities viz. ***sattva***, ***rajas*** and ***tamas***. Human beings express a combination of these qualities. Sattvic qualities are associated with calmness and wisdom, rajas with activity and restlessness, and tamas with dullness or apathy.
Guru	Spiritual teacher.

Guru Gītā — Sacred verses glorifying the Guru.

Hanumān — One of the foremost devotees of Rāma. He led an army of *vānaras* (monkeys) into Lanka, and helped to topple Rāvaṇa's regime.

haṭha yōga — Physical exercises or *āsanas* designed to enhance one's overall well-being by toning the body and opening the various channels of the body to promote the free flow of energy.

idam — 'This;' universe; used in Vēdantic discourses to refer to the object of all experience; distinguished from ***aham***.

īśvara-kṛpā — Divine grace.

Indra — Leader of the *dēvas* (gods), and God of rain and thunderstorms.

iṣṭa-dēvatā — Preferred form of divinity.

Janaka — Father of Sītā and ruler of Mithila.

jananam — Birth.

janma — same as ***jananam***; can be interpreted to mean the interlude between birth (*jananam*) and death (*maraṇam*).

japa	Repeated chanting of a mantra.
jīva / jīvātmā	Individual Self or Soul.
jñāna	Knowledge of the Truth.
jñāna mārga	Path of knowledge. In this path, the knowledge of the identity between Brahman and the Self dawns on the basis of hearing (*śravaṇa*), reflection (*manana*) and meditation (*nididhyāsana*).
jñānī	Knower of the Truth.
kadamba	*Neolamarckia cadamba*; an evergreen, tropical tree.
kaḷari	Generally, a center for martial arts training; here, it refers to a temple where Amma used to hold Kṛṣṇa Bhāva and Dēvī Bhāva darśans.
karma	Action; mental, verbal or physical activity.
karma yōga	The way of dedicated action, the path of selfless service.
Kāḷī	Goddess of fearsome aspect; depicted as dark, wearing a garland of skulls, and a girdle of human hands; feminine of Kāla (time).

Kaikēyī	One of King Daśaratha's three wives; mother of Bharata; instigated Rāma's exile from Ayōdhyā.
Kali Yuga	see ***yuga***.
kalpa	One day of Lord Brahmā; about 4.32 billion years; each kalpa is made up of 1,000 *mahāyugas*, and each *mahāyuga* is made up of four yugas. It spans the period from creation to dissolution; see ***yuga***.
kalpa-vṛkṣa	Mythical wish-fulfilling tree.
kāma	Lust, specifically; desire in general.
Kāmadhēnu	'Cow of plenty,' who provides the owner with whatever he/she desires.
Kamsa	Maternal uncle of Kṛṣṇa who overthrew his father and usurped the throne of Mathura.
kāmya bhakti	Devotion based on desire for an object; contrasted with ***tattvattilē bhakti***.
Kaṇvāśram	A spiritual center associated with Maharṣi Kaṇva.
Karṇa	One of the greatest warriors in the Mahābhārata War; though the son of Kuntī, the mother of the other

	Pāṇḍavas, he fought with Duryōdhana on the Kaurava side.
Kāśī	Also known as Vārāṇasī or Benāres; holy Indian city on the banks of River Ganga in the state of Uttar Pradēsh.
Kēśava	Name of Viṣṇu; one with long hair (*kēśa*); one who destroyed the demon Kēśi; therefore, one of Kṛṣṇa's epithets.
kīrtanam	Chanting the Lord's names; see ***nava-vidha-bhakti.***
krōdha	Anger.
kṛpā	Grace.
Kṛṣṇa	From '*kṛṣ*,' meaning 'to draw to oneself' or 'to remove sin;' principal incarnation of Lord Viṣṇu. He was born into a royal family but raised by foster parents, and lived as a cowherd boy in Vṛndāvan, where He was loved and worshipped by His devoted companions, the gōpīs and gōpas. Kṛṣṇa later established the city of Dwāraka. He was a friend and advisor to His cousins, the Pāṇḍavas, especially Arjuna, whom He served as charioteer during the Mahābhārata War, and to

	whom He revealed His teachings as the *Bhagavad Gītā*.
kumkum	Saffron powder; used as a religious mark (on the forehead) by the devout.
Kuntī	Mother of the Pāṇḍavas and Karṇa, and paternal aunt of Kṛṣṇa.
Kurukṣētra	Battlefield where the war between the Pāṇḍavas and Kauravas was fought; also, a metaphor for the conflict between good and evil.
Lakṣmaṇa	Younger brother of Rāma.
Lakṣmī	Goddess of wealth and prosperity, and consort of Viṣṇu.
līlā	Divine play.
Mā	'Mother;' in the meditation that Amma teaches, 'Mā' is the sound that one mentally synchronizes with every inhalation during the initial stages of meditation (before the sound dissolves into the breath).
Mahābali	A great ruler of demons, who attained God-realization through ***ātmanivēdanam*** (self-surrender).

Mahābhārata	Ancient Indian epic that Sage Vyāsa composed, depicting the war between the righteous Pāṇḍavas and the unrighteous Kauravas.
maharṣi	'Great (*mahā*) ṛṣi.' See ***ṛṣi***.
mahātmā	Literally, 'great soul.' Used to describe one who has attained spiritual realization.
Malayāḷam	Language spoken in the Indian state of Kēraḷa.
mānasa pūja	Ceremonial worship performed by visualization.
mantra	A sound, syllable, word or words of spiritual content. According to Vēdic commentators, mantras were revealed to ***ṛṣis*** while they were in deep meditation.
maraṇam	Death.
mauna	Silence; the cessation of thoughts or mental vacillations.
Māyā	Cosmic delusion, personified as a temptress. Illusion; appearance, as contrasted with Reality; the creative power of the Lord.
Mīnākṣī	Literally, one whose eyes are fish-shaped; a form of the Goddess. This form is

enshrined in a temple in Madurai; hence the sobriquet 'Madurai Mīnākṣī.'

Mēlpattūr Mēlpattūr Nārāyaṇa Bhaṭṭatiri was an erudite scholar who composed the ***Nārāyaṇīyam***.

mōn 'Son' in Malayāḷam

mṛdangam South Indian drum.

mūla mantra Root mantra associated with specific pujas in a temple.

nava-vidha-bhakti Nine modes of devotion, *viz.* *śravaṇam* (hearing the Lord's glory), *kīrtanam* (chanting the Lord's name), *smaraṇam* (remembering the Lord and His divine play), *pādasēvanam* (serving the Lord's feet), *arcanam* (worshipping the Lord), *vandanam* (prostrating to the Lord), *dāsyam* (becoming a servant of the Lord), *sakhyam* (becoming a friend of the Lord) and *ātmanivēdanam* (surrendering wholly to the Lord).

Nārada Wandering sage ever engaged in singing the praises of Viṣṇu. He composed the *Nārada Bhakti Sūtras*, aphorisms on devotion.

Nārāyaṇīyam	A Sānskṛt poem that summarizes the *Bhāgavata Purāṇa.*
ñāval	Black plum.
navarasa	In Indian art and dance, the nine aesthetic sentiments that are considered pure emotions.
nitya-mukta	Eternally free.
ōm	see ***aum***.
pādābhiṣēkam	Ceremonial washing of the feet.
pādasēvanam	Serving the Lord's feet; see ***nava-vidha-bhakti***.
Pāñcālī	See **Draupadi**.
Pāṇḍavas	Five sons of King Pāṇḍu, and cousins of Kṛṣṇa.
pappaṭam	Crisp, wafer-like Indian chips, typically of circular shape, made from lentil flour.
Paramātmā	Supreme Self.
Parīkṣit	Grandson of Arjuna. Owing to a rash act, he was cursed to die of snakebite. He spent the last week of his life listening to Śuka's enlightening spiritual discourses.

pīṭham	Low platform; seat for the Guru; a center of learning and power; a sacred place, as in Śakti Pīṭha.
prārabdha	The consequences of actions from previous lives that one is destined to experience in the present life.
prasād	Blessed offering or gift from a holy person or temple, often in the form of food.
prēyas	The pleasant, which detracts from one's spiritual well-being; often contrasted with ***śrēyas***.
pūja	Ritualistic or ceremonial worship.
Pūntānam	Pūntānam Nambūtiri, a poet, contemporary of Mēlpattūr, and devotee of Guruvāyūrappan, a manifestation of Lord Viṣṇu. Author of *Jñānappāna* ('Song of Wisdom'), written in Malayāḷam.
puṇya	Spiritual merit.
purāṇa puruṣa	Ancient being, yet ever fresh and new.
Purāṇas	Compendium of stories – including the biographies and stories of gods, saints, kings and great people – allegories and chronicles of great historical events that

aim to make the teachings of the Vēdas simple and available to all.

puruṣārtha The four-fold aims of human life, *viz.* ***dharma*** (virtuousness), ***artha*** (acquisition of material wealth), ***kāma*** (fulfillment of desire) and ***mōkṣa*** (spiritual liberation).

pūṭṭu South Indian breakfast item made from rice flour.

Rājasūya Yajña Grand and elaborate sacrifice performed in ancient India by kings who considered themselves sovereign rulers.

Rāma The divine hero of the epic *Rāmāyaṇa*. An incarnation of Lord Viṣṇu, He is considered the ideal man of *dharma* and virtue. '*Ram*' means 'to revel;' one who revels in Himself; the principle of joy within; also one who gladdens the hearts of others.

Ramaṇa Maharṣi

Enlightened spiritual master (1879 – 1950) who lived in Tiruvaṇṇāmalai in Tamiḷ Nāḍu. He recommended Self-inquiry as the path to Liberation,

	though He approved of a variety of paths and spiritual practices.
Rāmānuja	Hindu theologian, philosopher and exegete (1017 – 1137 CE), who was the leading exponent of ***Viśiṣṭādvaita***.
Rāmāyaṇa	A 24,000-verse epic poem on the life and times of Rāma.
rasa	An essential mental state; spiritual rapture; one of the nine classical emotions (***navarasa***).
Rāvaṇa	King of Lanka, and primary antagonist in the *Rāmāyaṇa*.
ṛṣi	Seer to whom mantras were revealed in deep meditation.
Śabarimala	Temple in Kēraḷa's Western Ghats dedicated to Lord Ayyappa.
Sadāśiva Brahmēndra	18th century saint, composer and Advaita philosopher.
sādhana	Regime of disciplined and dedicated spiritual practice that leads to the supreme goal of Self-realization.
sādhak	Spiritual aspirant or seeker.
sādhu	Holy person or spiritual aspirant.

sakhyam A mode of devotion in which the devotee regards God as a friend and companion; see ***nava-vidha-bhakti.***

sākṣi bhāva Witness attitude.

Śakti Power; personification of the Universal Mother; principle of pure energy associated with Śiva, the principle of pure consciousness.

Śaktibhadra A renowned poet from Kēraḷa who authored the Sānskṛt poem '*Āścarya Cūḍāmaṇi,*' and who was a contemporary of Ādi Śankarācārya.

Śākyamuni Literally, 'silent one of the Śakya clan,' an epithet of the Buddha.

śama Mind control.

samādhi Literally, 'cessation of all mental movements;' oneness with God; a transcendental state in which one loses all sense of individual identity; union with Absolute Reality; a state of intense concentration in which consciousness is completely unified.

samsāra Cycle of births and deaths; the world of flux; the wheel of birth, decay, death and rebirth.

samskāra	The totality of one's personality traits that one has acquired as a result of conditioning over many lifetimes. This can also be taken to mean one's level of inner refinement or character.
sankalpa	Divine resolve, usually used in association with mahātmās.
Sānskṛt	Ancient Indo-European language; the language of most ancient Hindu scriptures.
śānti	Spiritual peace.
sanyāsa	A formal vow of renunciation.
sanyāsī	A monk who has taken formal vows of renunciation (sanyāsa); traditionally wears an ocher-colored robe, representing the burning away of all desires. The female equivalent is *sanyāsinī*.
Saraswatī	Goddess of Learning and the Arts.
śāstra	Science; in the context of this book, authoritative scriptural texts.
satsang	Being in communion with the Supreme Truth. Also being in the company of *mahātmās*, studying scriptures, listening to a spiritual talk or discussion, and

	participating in spiritual practices in a group setting.
sattva	See ***guṇa***.
sēva	Selfless service, the results of which are dedicated to God.
śīrṣāsana	Headstand.
Sītā	Rāma's holy consort. In India, She is considered the ideal of womanhood.
Śiva	Worshipped as the first and the foremost in the lineage of Gurus, and as the formless substratum of the universe in relationship to Śakti. He is the Lord of destruction in the Trinity of Brahmā (Lord of Creation), Viṣṇu (Lord of Sustenance), and Mahēśvara (Śiva).
smaraṇam	Remembering the Lord and His divine play; see ***nava-vidha-bhakti***.
śraddhā	Attentiveness; faith.
śravaṇam	Hearing the Lord's glory (see ***nava-vidha-bhakti)***; different from śravaṇa in ***jñāna mārga***.
śrēyas	The good, which conduces to the spiritual well-being of a person; often contrasted with ***prēyas***.

Śrī A title of respect originally meaning 'divine,' 'holy' or 'auspicious;' now in modern India, simply a respectful form of address, similar to 'Mr.'

Śrī Laḷitā Aṣṭōttaram
Sacred litany of the 108 attributes of Śrī Laḷitā Dēvī, the Supreme Goddess.

Śrī Laḷitā Sahasranāma
Sacred litany of 1,000 names of Śrī Laḷitā Dēvī, the Supreme Goddess.

Śrī Laḷitā Triśatī
Sacred litany of 300 names of Śrī Laḷitā Dēvī, the Supreme Goddess.

Śrīmad Bhāgavatam
Also known as *Bhāgavatam* or *Bhāgavata Purāṇa* (meaning 'Sacred Tales of the Supreme Lord'), one of the Purāṇic texts of Hinduism. Contains stories of the incarnations of Viṣṇu, including the life and pastimes of Kṛṣṇa.

Śrī Rāmakṛṣṇa Paramahamsa
A 19th century spiritual master from West Bengal, hailed as the apostle of religious harmony. He generated a

	spiritual renaissance that continues to touch the lives of millions.
sthita-prajñā	Person of steady wisdom.
sudarśana cakra	A spinning, disk-like weapon; associated with Lord Viṣṇu.
Śuka	Son of Vyāsa and main narrator of the ***Bhāgavatam***.
swāmi	Title of one who has taken the vow of ***sanyāsa***.
Swāmi Rāma Tīrtha	The most notable teacher of Vēdānta to preach in the West after Swāmi Vivēkānanda.
Swāmi Vivēkānanda	Chief monastic disciple of Śrī Rāmakṛṣṇa Paramahamsa.
Syamantaka	Mythological gem with magical powers.
tabla	Pair of hand drums, associated with the traditional music of the Indian subcontinent.
tapas	Austerity, penance.
tattvattilē bhakti	Devotion based on an understanding of spiritual principles; contrasted with ***kāmya bhakti***.

Tiruvaḷḷuvar Tamil poet and philosopher, most famous for the *Tirukkuraḷ*, a work on *dharma*, *artha* (wealth) and *kama* (desire).

Trētā Yuga see ***yuga***.

triguṇas see ***guṇa***.

Tryambaka Literally, 'three-eyed;' a name of Śiva, who is three-eyed and father of the three worlds; Śiva's bow, which Rāma successfully strung and broke to win the hand of Sītā in marriage.

Umā Another name for Pārvatī, consort of Lord Śiva; Divine Mother.

upadēśa Spiritual advice.

Upaniṣad The portions of the Vēdas dealing with Self-knowledge.

vairāgya Dispassion.

Vaḷḷikkāvu Village across the backwaters on the eastern side of the peninsula where the Amṛtapuri Āśram is located. Amma is sometimes referred to as 'Vaḷḷikkāvu Amma.'

vandanam	Salutation; prostrating to the Lord; see ***nava-vidha-bhakti***.
Vārāṇasī	see **Kāśī**.
Varkala	Coastal town in the district of Tiruvanantapuram in Kēraḷa.
vāsanā	Latent tendency or subtle desire that manifests as thought, motive and action; subconscious impression gained from experience.
Vasiṣṭha	Great sage and Guru of Rāma.
Vasudēva	Father of Kṛṣṇa.
Vāsuki	Snake that the gods and demons utilized to work the churning rod, which was used to obtain the nectar of immortality from the ocean of milk; wife of Tiruvaḷḷuvar.
Vāyu	Wind God and presiding deity of touch.
Vēdānta	'The end of the Vēdas.' It refers to the Upaniṣads, which deal with the subject of Brahman, the Supreme Truth, and the path to realize that Truth.
Vēdāntin	Follower or practitioner of Vēdānta.
Vēdas	Most ancient of all scriptures, originating from God, the Vēdas were not composed by any human author but were 'revealed'

	in deep meditation to the ancient ṛṣis. These sagely revelations came to be known as Vēdas, of which there are four: Ṛg, Yajus, Sāma and Atharva.
Vēdic	Of or pertaining to the ancient Vēdas.
Vēṇu	Author's pre-monastic name.
vibhakti	Scholarship.
Viśiṣṭādvaita	'Qualified Advaita.' Philosophy that holds that Brahman alone exists. The *jīva* (individual soul) and *jagat* (universe) are manifestations or attributes of Brahman.
Viṣṇu	Lord of Sustenance in the Hindu Trinity.
Vyāsa	Father of Śuka, compiler of the Vēdas, and author of the *Purāṇas*, *Brahmasūtras*, *Mahābhārata* and the *Śrīmad Bhāgavatam*.
vyatirēka	Negation, discordance or difference; distinction, separateness, exclusion; often contrasted with ***anvaya***.
Yaśodā	Foster mother of Kṛṣṇa.
yōga	From '*yuj*' (*samādhau*), which means 'to concentrate the mind;' '*yuj*' (*samyamanē*), which means 'to control;' and '*yujir*' (*yōgē*), which means 'to unite.' Union

with the Supreme Being. A broad term, it also refers to the various methods of practices through which one can attain oneness with the Divine. A path that leads to Self-realization.

yōganidrā Yōgic sleep in which there is absolute awareness.

yuga According to Hindu cosmogony, the universe (from origin to dissolution) passes through a cycle made up of four Yugas or ages. The first is Kṛta Yuga, during which dharma reigns in society. Each succeeding age sees the progressive decline of dharma. The second age is known as Trētā Yuga, the third is Dvāpara Yuga, and the fourth and present epoch is known as Kali Yuga.

pronunciation guide

Vowels can be short or long:

a – as ‘u’ in but

ā – as ‘a’ in far

e – as ‘a’ in may

ē – as ‘a’ in name

i – as ‘i’ in pin

ī – as ‘ee’ in meet

o – as in oh

ō – as ‘o’ in mole

u – as ‘u’ in push

ū – as ‘oo’ in hoot

ṛ – as ri in rim

ḥ – pronounce ‘aḥ’ like ‘aha,’ ‘iḥ’ like ‘ihi,’ and ‘uḥ’ like ‘uhu.’

Some consonants are aspirated (e.g. kh); others are not (e.g. k). The aspiration is part of the consonant. The examples given below are therefore only approximate.

k – as ‘k’ in ‘kite’

kh – as ‘ckh’ in ‘Eckhart’

g – as ‘g’ in ‘give’

gh – as ‘g-h’ in ‘dig-hard’

c – as ‘c’ in ‘cello’

ch – as ‘ch-h’ in ‘staunch-heart’

j – as ‘j’ in ‘joy’

jh – as ‘dgeh’ in ‘hedgehog’

ñ – as ‘ny’ in ‘canyon’

The letters d, t, n with dots under them are pronounced with the tip of the tongue against the roof of the mouth, the others with the tip against the teeth.

ṭ – as ‘t’ in ‘tub’

ṭh – as ‘th’ in ‘lighthouse’

ḍ – as ‘d’ in ‘dove’

ḍh – as ‘dh’ in ‘red-hot’

ṇ – as ‘n’ in ‘naught’

p – as ‘p’ in ‘pine’

ph – as ‘ph’ in ‘up-hill’

b – as ‘b’ in ‘bird’

bh – as ‘bh’ in ‘rub-hard’

m – as ‘m’ in ‘mother’

y – as ‘y’ in ‘yes’

r – as ‘r’ in Italian ‘Roma’ (rolled)

ḷ – as ‘l’ in ‘like’

v – as w in ‘when’

ṣ – as ‘sh’ in ‘shine’

ś – as 's' in German 'sprechen'

s – as 's' in 'sun'

h – as 'h' in 'hot'

With double consonants the initial sound only is pronounced twice:

cc – as 'tc' in 'hot chip'

jj – as 'dj' in 'red jet'

The 'ऽ' sign has been used when the vowel 'a' has been elided. For example, the word '*śivōऽham*' is a compound of '*śivaḥ*' and 'aham.' When these words are conjoined, the initial vowel in 'aham' is elided, and the elision is indicated by the 'ऽ' sign.

about the author

Swāmi Praṇavāmṛtānanda Puri joined the āśram in 1980 and is one of Amma's senior-most sanyāsī disciples. He holds a B.Sc. degree in Zoology and an M.A. in Sānskṛt Literature. In accordance with Amma's instructions, Swāmiji has been teaching Sānskṛt to the āśram residents. He is also a featured speaker on the Amrita TV channel. A reputed singer and percussionist, Swāmiji has accompanied Amma to various programs in India and abroad. He has written and scored many devotional songs. Swāmiji is the author of '*My Mother, My Master*' (English) and '*Amma nalkiya pāṭhangaḷ*' (Malayāḷam). This is his third book.

CPSIA information can be obtained
at www.ICGtesting.com
Printed in the USA
LVOW03s1908210517
535206LV00004B/8/P

9 781680 377064